CRYSTAL
SHAMANISM

SACRED EARTH
MEDICINE HEALINGS

RACHELLE CHARMAN

ROCKPOOL

A Rockpool book
PO Box 252
Summer Hill
NSW 2130
Australia

rockpoolpublishing.com
Follow us! **f** 🄾 rockpoolpublishing
Tag your images with #rockpoolpublishing

Published in 2023 by Rockpool Publishing
ISBN: 9781925924954

Design and typesetting by Sara Lindberg, Rockpool Publishing
Edited by Lisa Macken

A catalogue record for this
book is available from the
National Library of Australia

Printed and bound in China
10 9 8 7 6 5 4 3 2 1

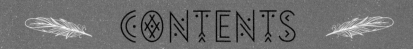

CONTENTS

INTRODUCTION

I would like to begin by acknowledging the Traditional Custodians of the land on which you read this book and ask that you join me in paying respects to their Elders past and present and future generations.

My path has led me down a deeply healing and life-changing journey, and I have been blessed to have connected with some very special souls, traditional shamans and spiritual leaders over the years. The door first opened when I had a powerful soul awakening with an amethyst crystal, which then led me to manifest a job at Hay House Publishing working as Doreen Virtue's personal assistant and mentor to thousands of angel initiatives. My heart then guided me on an adventure around the world and meeting shamans from different cultures, which allowed me to birth and connect deeply with my own shamanic teachings and wisdom. I spent 20 years, from 2000 to 2020, running my own academy of healing, sharing my stories and guiding healers to connect with their own personal medicine and supporting them to share it with the world. Over that time more than 10,000 students and 50 teachers came through the door. I have continued to travel the world

facilitating workshops on crystals, shamanism, drum making, inner child and Pleiadian healing, offering this sacredness to whoever feels the calling.

I invite you to take a journey with me as we uncover the secrets that have led me to this sacred work and the awakening of my own personal soul's medicine.

The information, ceremonies and healings found in this book are not from any specific lineage but are birthed from my own connection with each medicine and my own personal awakening and remembering. I offer this book to you as an initiation from my soul to yours and invite you to open and receive the ancient downloads of energy contained within. The book and its contents are sacred, and I ask that you treat them accordingly. As you embark upon this journey and read through the book, actively working with the processes, know you will enter into a vortex and sacred space just as though you were sitting with a shaman or visiting a sacred site. As you read you will activate a powerful energy that is offered to you for the highest good of all and with the highest form of love possible. There is no mistake that you have been guided to connect with this book and its sacred teachings. Possibly we have a soul contract in this life and my part is to offer this sacred space for you to remember and discover your own shamanic wisdom.

The intention of this book is to offer inspiration and be an invitation to rekindle your own connection with this beautiful earth, her allies, energies, great spirit and your own personal medicine. Many of us are awakening ancient shamanic wisdom from within, wisdom held in our DNA from our ancestors and our past-life experiences as medicine people. All of this information is available now and can be activated at will, so it's time for you to awaken to your inner shaman and embody this power in your own life. Please take what feels right and leave what doesn't and, most importantly, allow my story and the shamanic wisdom to spark and awaken your own truth and powerful medicine. This offering is from my heart to yours, and that you are here in this moment reading these words means that you are a powerful medicine person.

I hope to invite a fresh perspective on shamanism while at the same time honouring all ancient law and culture and respecting the sacredness of the old ways, stories and ceremonies. I believe we are all native to this land called Mother Gaia, and that some of us have soul contracts to share our medicine utilising the old ways while creating new ceremony and integrating fresh

practices. The calling and passion to do so is driven from a need to heal and bring our land and her people into a state of balance, harmony and peace.

I truly hope that me sharing these stories opens you up to see that you have shamanic medicine within you, whether it is in this lifetime, a past life or your ancestors: somewhere in your soul there has been a deep connecting with shamanism. If you have a yearning then it's time to awaken, to look after this earth, each other and yourself and it's time to create new ceremonies and bring back the sacred. I truly hope the wisdom and medicine in this book inspires you to awaken to your shamanic gifts.

HOW TO WORK WITH THIS BOOK

Over the last 20 years I created a range of powerful healing processes that I use in my healing business and offer in my workshops. Most of the healing processes you will find in this book are what I teach in my Crystal Shamanism levels 1 and 2 workshops. I invite you to utilise the healings for yourself or work with them in your healing practice. However, if you choose to offer them to others make sure you have experienced them yourself and that you thoroughly understand the medicine.

The chapters of the book begin with an outline of the subject of the chapter and some healing earth medicine processes you can utilise for yourself or offer to others. After that I offer my personal experience and awakening of the medicine. Next I relate which crystals guided me to awaken to my knowledge, crystals that worked as allies to assist me in building a strong relationship with the spirit of each medicine. Finally, I offer you a healing process or ceremony so you can have your own experience. Some of the healings are advanced processes, so it's very important that you embody and understand the medicine before you offer it to others.

Part III runs through all of the important steps of healing for practitioners and has a healing code of conduct. If you choose to offer healings to other people, please ensure you read this key section of the book.

Note: when you see the words 'Personal healing' it refers to a meditation, process, healing or ceremony you do with yourself, while 'Practitioner healing' refers to a meditation, process, healing or ceremony you facilitate for someone else.

PART I

SHAMANISM

CHAPTER 1

AWAKENING YOUR INNER SHAMAN

I was born and raised in the city, and my connection with Mother Earth and her medicine and my shamanic gifts were never taught to me by my parents or anyone in my sphere of influence in my younger years. My journey into shamanism came from a natural awareness that was sparked within and my own personal experiences as I walked the path of healing. I definitely had guidance and support from some very special people along the way, but the majority of my shamanic connection came through my own inquiry.

I have had many moments of awareness of being a shaman in a past life and have been given the opportunity to bring this energy and my gifts into this life. Mother Earth with her powerful medicines and my team in the spirit world facilitated many healings and initiations so I could understand the medicine intimately. The more I connected with myself the more connected I felt with my surroundings and the wisdom of shamanic

practices. There were times when I would have amazing experiences and then receive confirmations in books and conversations that what I was awakening to was ancient shamanic healing processes. How could I have this knowledge, and who was I to have these experiences?

Something really sacred and special was happening to me, something beyond my comprehension. I was invited to trust and allow a deep awakening to occur, and so I did. It was like waking up from a deep sleep to an ancient wisdom from the beginning of time. I came to understand that we are all connected with this beautiful earth and all her medicines and I believe it's everyone's birthright to understand this union. This awakening is a personal journey and powerful vision quest through life.

We are currently living in a very special time, when as a race and mass consciousness we are awakening to a deeper truth. I believe the veils of the worlds are at their thinnest and the ability to access ancient wisdom is abundant. This knowing is in our blood and bones, our DNA, and it's in our souls, and we are currently in a global awakening to this deeper truth. People are starting to wake up, to question the main narrative and delve deep within their own souls for guidance and healing. Religions are being questioned, and the development of modern-day medicine appears to be stagnant.

People are looking for alternative ways of living and a deeper connection and truth, and are turning to shamanism and back to the old natural ways of the land for guidance and answers. The shamans have understood this connection from the beginning of time, and I believe we are shamans who have been birthed back into this world to help humanity. We are rainbow bridges offering fresh wisdom and new ceremonies to assist society and Mother Earth as we come together to create an alternative way forward, one that doesn't destroy or harm the planet and all who inhabit her but instead allows us to live in harmony with nature and the law of the land in balance and with love at the core.

It is time to awaken this innate knowing inside of us and offer it in our present time to our community and those who feel lost and in need of guidance and healing. We are the wounded healers and we are driven and inspired to help others through our own life challenges and diversity. You are one of these people and it is time to listen to your own inner calling and birth your light on this planet; it is time to awaken your ancient inner shaman. This wisdom is within you – it always has been and always will be – and it's time to bring it forth and birth it into reality for the greater good of the planet and the divine healing of all.

Your powerful spirit has guided you to this moment and will continue to support and direct you on your path. Trust your inner calling. I am so happy that you have arrived at this moment in time. Life hasn't been easy for you, and you have made it. My heart and soul honours your heart and soul for all that you have been through and all that you are.

This book is for anyone drawn to the path of healing or helping humanity or who has an interest in shamanism and earth medicine. You can simply read this book or you can delve deeply into your soul and awaken to your powerful truth: the choice is yours. This constant awakening leads us down a path of walking gently on this land to be the best possible version of ourselves and sparks a deep fire inside to guide others on their path of self-love and healing. I invite you to take this shamanic journey with me, walking side by side, and will share many stories and wisdom that has opened me up profoundly to earth wisdom and offer processes that will assist you to awaken, trust and follow your own path of shamanism.

Let's begin this journey together.

THE MEDICINE OF SHAMANISM

A shaman is the healer or medicine person of a tribe, the one who holds the wisdom and creates healing, ceremony and rites of passage for their community. Shamans walk between the worlds, one foot in reality and the other in non-reality states of consciousness. They experience and invoke trance-like states that allow them to journey into the spirit worlds to access powerful energy and medicine for people who seek healing. They work with the medicine of the earth and spirit and know them both intimately.

The three shamanic paths

Although there are three main ways to embark upon the shamanic path, no matter what path awakens you to your shamanic roots they all lead you to the same destination of working deeply and sacredly with the medicine of the earth and the spiritual realms. You learn to walk with one foot in both worlds and become the conduit and medium between them.

The first way to journey the shamanic path and the traditional way is to be born into a family of shamans and be chosen to continue the ancestral wisdom from previous generations. The shaman of the family watches the young ones growing up to see if they show any traits of a shaman. If they do the shaman takes that young person under their wing and teaches them their sacred craft and the secret ways of their people. The young person spends many years in training, going through countless ceremonies and rites of passages to ensure they are ready and fit for the job.

The second way to journey the shamanic path is an internal calling to a particular lineage, one in which you devote your life to a specific tradition and make your way through the teachings and initiations with the intention of mastering the craft. You would spend time with a master of this medicine learning how to fully embody the shamanic processes and wisdom.

The third way to journey the shamanic path and the way in which many these days are finding shamanism is through a soul awakening or dark night of the soul. This is usually invoked by some type of personal trauma such as sickness or a mental health crisis in which you are called to look deeper within yourself for the answers. As I mentioned before, we are living in a time when many are waking up from a deep sleep to a birthing that is happening inside us, in our souls, in our DNA, a want to do better and help others in this world. This birthing can invoke memories of being a shaman in another time and place and open the veils of the worlds to a place where we are able to access this wisdom at will more than ever before.

Similarities between traditional and modern-day shamanism

In traditional shamanism the shaman enters into a trance-like state and journeys into other realms to gather healing energy to bring back and offer to others for healing. Modern-day healers or shamans drop into deep meditation and bring through healing energy for their clients. Although it is a slightly different process, the intention and outcome are the same.

Traditional shamans connect with the spirits of many different earthly medicines and offer this energy to others for healing. Modern-day shamans work with the same medicine; for example, crystals to assist others and themselves in healing.

Traditional shamans lived away from the tribe and were seen as being slightly mad or eccentric. Modern-day shamans usually feel like the black sheep of the family or the odd one out. It is the same essence, just played out slightly differently due to our contemporary age.

There are many similarities between the healers of today and ancient shamans: they all access the same source to create healing and awakening for themselves and others. A shaman or healer's intention is to bring balance and healing to the mind, emotions, physical body and spirit, with the ultimate goal being to create powerful healing for the soul. By finding your own connection with the god source, spirit, earth and its healing medicines and tools you will start to awaken your inner shaman and truly understand this amazing world we live in, the universe and the power of love and healing.

MY PERSONAL EXPERIENCE

On my shamanic path I have been truly blessed to have received several initiations from shamans and medicine people around the globe, but I don't believe you need to be initiated by others because this wisdom is inside you and the gifts from past lives as shamans is awakening within you. However, at different times of the journey you may meet someone who assists in activating this energy within you or you may be drawn to certain places on the planet – vortexes – that also hold this energy to assist you to awaken. Fundamentally, it is within you. A part of my awakening and soul contract was to meet up with certain souls to assist me on my journey, and I would love to share some of my story and how I awoke to my own shamanic wisdom and deep connection with our earth and her powerful medicine.

Despite not being guided onto this shamanic path in my early years and my traditional Catholic upbringing, it was still an organic and natural part of my journey to start becoming aware of this more shamanic aspect within myself. After my time working with Doreen Virtue and Hay House Australia and connecting deeply with all the angelic energies, I felt it was time to understand and connect with the new energy that was stirring within me.

I started to become aware of a deep inner calling to travel to Peru and I felt a strong knowing that I was going to meet a very powerful shaman. I decided to listen to the calling and went travelling around the world, spending six months living in South America. It was one of the most challenging but also amazing times of my life; I felt as though I had stepped into James Redfield's novel *The Celestine Prophecy*, about one person's journey to understand spiritual insights.

I had been in Cusco in the Peruvian Andes for just a few days when I felt my soul stirring, and I was constantly asking myself when and how I was going to find the sacred man. One afternoon I was in the foyer of my hotel writing in my diary when a group of people entered the room. Excitement and electricity filled my body as I knew one of the Peruvian men in the group was the man I was waiting for, the one I had travelled there to meet. I creepily stared at him and his friend for ages before they calmly walked over to my table.

They spoke to each other in Quechua, the native Peruvian language, then one of the men turned to me and said: 'The angel you are looking for is within.' His name was Jesús, and he was the friend and interpreter of the other man, Edwin, who I later found out is my shaman. Edwin's words through Jesús completely blew me away, especially after just having spent many years working with Doreen Virtue and the angels. I took these words as a strong sign and confirmation that I was exactly where I was meant to be. I knew deep in my soul my heart had guided me to this perfect moment in time: Edwin was the man I had been searching for. Jesús and Edwin joined me at my table, and Edwin said that he had known I was coming and that we had a soul contract in this life.

Edwin was a gentle, beautiful soul and powerful medicine man whose mother was hit by lightning when she was pregnant with him and taken to their community's shaman. When Edwin was young he was also hit by lightning and taken to the same shaman. In the Peruvian tradition, being hit by lightning is a sign from the gods and ancestors as an initiation into shamanism, so the shaman chose Edwin to hand on his ancient ways and wisdom to.

Me at Machu Picchu.

I lived on and off with Edwin and his family for months, during which time he took me on journeys to sacred places and we shared many initiations and ceremonies. Edwin didn't speak English and I didn't speak Quechua so the time we shared was in silence, but I quickly realised our union went beyond language and felt a deep heart connection to this beautiful man. I had finally manifested a teacher whom I didn't put on a pedestal or give away my power to and one who walked beside me, guiding and encouraging me to have my own experience and awaken to my own intuitive knowing.

It took years to fully integrate the work we did together; however, it awoke something deep inside me, something that was familiar and that I had known previously in another time and space. I learned to completely trust working with Edwin, who would turn up at all hours of the morning and take me on trips into the Andes. We undertook ceremonies and initiations and spent time connecting deeply with the land and the ancient teaching of the Andes.

Most of the sacred and special places in Peru are hidden or nestled on top of mountains. One time we drove for hours to get to a sacred valley. We parked the car in the middle of nowhere and started to walk up a huge mountain, and when we reached the top Edwin guided me into a cave. He picked up a stone from the floor, placed it into my palm and signed for me to close my eyes. I thought I was the luckiest person alive, being on top of a mountain in Peru with my shaman doing ceremony, and I felt so blessed. After a considerable amount of time had gone by I opened my eyes to realise Edwin was no longer there. I quickly went from feeling euphoric to being scared that I'd been left alone on top of a mountain in Peru. No one knew I was there and I started to panic.

Just before I was about to totally lose it, Edwin walked in with a smile on his face like he knew what was happening. He led me down to the river, where he picked up a stone from the water and placed it into my hand. He left me to connect with this energy of water. After a while he returned and we made a fire together, where we created a medicine prayer bundle and finished by offering the bundle to the fire as he gave me a condor feather blessing. I didn't really have any idea at the time what we were doing, but on reflection I realised Edwin was guiding me and teaching me to connect with the elements. At first I was offered the opportunity to sit in the cave, which was in the womb of Mother Earth.

When we connect so deeply with the mother our mother wounds can arise for healing, which is why my issues of abandonment came to the surface and I was given a powerful opportunity to receive healing from Mother Earth. Being in the cave meant I was being invited to sit in her womb and receive the healing she was offering me. My experience with the water brought an awareness that water is cleansing, soothing and healing, and burning our prayers in the fire gave me an awareness of transformation,

power and rebirth. The blessing of the condor connected with the element of air and the understanding that this element was the messenger that guided energy from one place to the next and was offering my prayers to great spirit.

This was the start of my awakening to the power of the elements, and over the years I have gained a broader and deeper understanding of this medicine that I will share in the pages of this book. This earth medicine is always available to us; it is our birthright to deepen our relationship with it. Most of us are not taught this; however, it is rich within us and is just waiting for us to allow this connection. It is a neutral and organic rite of passage: we are all connected deeply with this earth and it's our birthright to work with, take care of and connect with Mother Earth and her medicines. If this city girl can awaken to this wisdom then anyone can. We all can, if our soul is calling.

CRYSTAL ALLY

NUUMMITE

Nuummite deeply connected me to my inner shaman, invited me to look within and trust and embody my shamanic healing wisdom and gifts on a whole new level. I was able to integrate my past-life experiences and draw on ancient wisdom in the present. Nuummite:

    ⫷ awakens the shaman within

    ⫷ supports you on the journey into your shadow self, creating a sacred space in which to obtain deep wisdom, strength and courage

    ⫷ increases strength and endurance during difficult times

    ⫷ assists you on the journey to self-mastery.

YOUR CEREMONY

This powerful mirror exercise will help you to increase your belief in yourself and own your shamanic gifts.

- Close your eyes and place a nuummite crystal on your heart. If you don't have one, use a photo or picture of nuummite.
- Call in the deva of the crystal and ask to be showered in its energy. Breathe this energy into your heart for a few minutes.
- Open your eyes and look at yourself in a mirror, then say three times: 'I am a powerful medicine woman/man.'
- Repeat this exercise morning and night for three consecutive days.

Record your experience.

_____

_____

_____

_____

_____

_____

_____

_____

_____

_____

_____

CHAPTER 2

SACRED CEREMONIES

Most tribes throughout history practised sacred ceremonies as a way to connect with and honour their ancestors, the land, each other, the gods and spirits and divine source. Ceremonies were also undertaken to strengthen the connection of the tribe with the earth so they could receive her wisdom and guidance.

THE MEDICINE OF SACRED CEREMONIES

Ceremonies are facilitated for many reasons such as rites of passage, passing over, marriage, initiation, celebration, healing, honouring the earth, moon cycles, planting seasons, honouring ancestors and spirit and to set intentions. They create healing energy that is shared with the people and the earth and all that inhabits her. They are a form of prayer or ritual that brings powerful and potent energy into sacred space and to those who are connected with the ceremony.

At ceremonies, which can last for weeks, people dance, sing, play instruments and dress up in ceremonial costumes, all to invoke the spirits. They are a huge celebration of existence and co-creation with all that is: past, present and future.

Ceremony is a huge part of life and is a missing piece of the puzzle in modern-day society. It facilitates a sense of belonging and connection, and without it we can get lost in the craziness of the world and everything around us.

It's time to initiate more ceremonies and rites of passage to help people feel as though they are a part of something, to feel honoured and seen so they have a deeper respect for and belief in themselves. Ceremonies will encourage people to act for the greater good of humanity and all that is and feel held, supported and guided through life, creating a deep sense of self, confidence and purpose.

MY PERSONAL EXPERIENCE

Jeremy Donovan in ceremony at the Sacred Journey Within retreat.

Around 10 years after my time with Edwin I had an experience that truly put me on my shamanic path and led me to birth my crystal shaman workshops and the wisdom in this book. I had an intense calling to run a retreat and bring together all of my favourite people from whom I had received healing over the previous 10 years. A three-day retreat held in Sydney with more than 100 participants, it was called Sacred Journey Within. An incredible amount of healing happened for so many people on this retreat, although there was one personal experience that particularly affected me on every level of my being that I still to this day keep sacred to my heart.

Jeremy, a dear friend and soul brother whom I met at Hay House, was one of the amazing facilitators at the retreat who shared their medicine. Jeremy is a Kuku Yalanji man who has an Aboriginal father and white Australian mum. Disconnected from culture and lore as a child, Jeremy found his family while incarcerated as a teenager but returned to Country at the age of 18. His First Nations grandfather reached out to him then took him to his land in Far North Queensland and taught him the ways of their people. The grandfather's medicine was the didgeridoo, and he handed this gift down to his grandson. Jeremy shared with me many experiences he had had with his grandfather, and it seemed to me that his grandfather was setting Jeremy up to be a conduit for his work in this world after the grandfather's passing.

When Jeremy was in ceremony throughout the retreat I felt and heard his grandfather come through in his energy and words, creating and offering a profound sacred space. After an incredible three days the retreat was coming to a close and we all gathered for the last ceremony. Jeremy had asked me if he could facilitate the closing ceremony, and I had felt honoured for him to do so. Everyone sat in a circle, and as there was so much love in the room the energy was that of a big happy family.

At the end of the ceremony Jeremy invited me to stand up in front of everyone, then took me by both hands and walked me around the circle. I could feel energy rise from within me like that of an erupting volcano and was later told that I had let out a huge squeal, which is unusual behaviour for me. However, my soul must have felt what was about to come. Jeremy guided me into the centre of the circle where he painted my

face with ochre, a sacred stone Indigenous people use to paint themselves in ceremony (their belief is that when ochre dries it is Mother Earth giving them a loving hug). As Jeremy started to play the didgeridoo, the energy was so intense I fell to the ground. It was a profound experience; I felt as though it was a rite of passage and he was honouring me for who I am and the things I do in this world. It was a blessing of my soul.

Jeremy handed me a piece of ochre rock from his medicine pouch and said: 'This was the only gift from my grandfather to me and now this is a gift from my grandfather to you.' I received the sacred gift and sobbed deep tears of gratitude, and there was not a dry eye in the circle; everyone could feel the sacredness of the situation and also received a blessing. The energy was truly sacred and like nothing I had ever felt before. Everyone held hands and closed the space with an 'Om'. The sound of the 'Om' turned to Indigenous women singing, and I could hear the sound of the didgeridoo coming out of the ground.

I felt as though I was an old Indigenous woman and that everyone at the retreat was my family: my children, my grandchildren and great-grandchildren from a past life. The experience sparked a profound connection with a lifetime as an Indigenous woman which in turn sparked a deep connection with the land and my shamanic medicine. As I said goodbye to everyone I knew without a doubt they had been my family in a past life and we were and always would be kin.

As we packed up the retreat all I wanted to do was lie down on the land, as I could feel it calling me from deep within. I could feel Jeremy's grandfather communicating with me in spirit, sharing many things. One powerful thing he told me was that my name in the past life was Running Water. I was truly in another world after the experience and had to try to pull myself out of it so I could return to my day-to-day life. I was walking on cloud nine and totally caught between the veils of the world and the timelines of my life. The day after the retreat I awoke thinking that something profound had happened to me. I could feel a connection with the earth deeper than I'd ever felt before and was in a complete space of love.

A dear friend who had been a presenter at the event called me that morning. Due to my ease in manifesting money her nickname for me had been 'Richie Rich', but she said quite unexpectedly that she now had to call

me Running Water. I couldn't believe my ears: she had just called me by the name Jeremy's grandfather had shared with me. What were the odds? This was a huge confirmation on many levels, and it helped me realise I wasn't crazy. I remember thinking to myself: what the hell happened last night in the ceremony? What did Jeremy do to me?

I was profoundly affected in a very positive way but I had no idea what had happened. All I wanted to do was talk to Jeremy; however, after the retreat he had headed over to the USA for a didgeridoo event. The next minute my phone rang and it was him: he had just landed and needed to talk with me. I asked him what had happened the previous night. He said he had no idea but that it had been powerful, and he also said he had only witnessed energy like that with his grandfather. He told me I was his family and that his grandfather was my grandfather.

It took years for me to integrate this experience, but it accelerated my journey into shamanism and allowed me to share my medicine with you within the pages of this book. I still to this day work with Jeremy's grandfather and feel him guiding and supporting me from the spirit world.

After the energy of the retreat settled I felt a little lost. I felt so connected to my Aboriginal past life and Jeremy's grandfather and had a deep calling to head north to the land of my ancestors in that life, which I believed was Jeremy's family. The universe always answers the calling, and I found out that Jeremy was planning a tour north to his ancestor's land. I was definitely in for the ride: this opportunity was a blessing as I really needed to find clarity and peace around what was going on in my life.

I had started to work with a new crystal, nuummite, that had come into my life so I decided to take it with me on a trip north. I discovered on the plane that a friend of a friend was sitting in the aisle across from me, and after a few minutes I leant over and said to him, 'Have a look at my beautiful crystal.' At the same time he said, 'Look at this crystal,' and we both opened our hands to show the nuummite sitting on our palms. They were the same size and shape, and we just looked at each other and knew we were in the right place and that nuummite would be facilitating the journey for us.

My time in Queensland was incredible in so many ways although it was also confronting and difficult to be on the land away from the

comforts of home, sitting with my emotions and thoughts and not having anything to distract me. We spent the entire time without shoes – so that our soles were in direct contact with the soul of the land – and living off the land, sleeping in swags and really connecting with nature in a raw way. We visited Jeremy's grandfather's grave and spent time on his land in Cape Tribulation. We discovered crystals that I was permitted to keep and made friends with some very sacred trees. One night we had a corroboree, for which we were painted in ochre and danced under the moon for hours.

Being on sacred land had allowed me to understand a deeper truth, but I still felt a disconnection and realised I was quite sick: I was overweight and unhappy with who I was. It was a hard realisation but at the same time one that probably saved my life. I then had this awareness that raised many questions. What am I searching for? Who am I? Why do I constantly look outside myself for answers and recognition? I was up north to find my Aboriginal ancestors and understood that I was still searching outside. I came to realise on a very deep level that no matter what you are looking for the answer is always within.

I knew it was time for some deep inner enquiry and to start trusting the guidance of my own soul, life lessons and wisdom, to love and be kind to myself on a deeper level and to let go of the old things that were keeping me stuck in a pattern of unworthiness. It was time to believe in myself like never before, so I started to unravel the connection with my past life as an Aboriginal woman and what it was teaching me in this lifetime. I had felt as though I was an Indigenous woman stuck in a white woman's body; I had fully embodied the past life and had one foot in both lifetimes.

There were times when I felt ashamed to be white and would question who I was to connect with the land and shamanic energy when I was not native to the land. I had a deep wound of not belonging that created a strange belief that white people don't have the right to connect to land that is not of their heritage. I felt I had no right being a white woman and doing ceremony and connecting with Mother Earth; however, at the same time I felt a profound connection to this country and the wisdom that was coming through from my past life. Within me I had two powerful aspects and parts of me were fighting against each other.

I didn't want this shame and pain to stop me from connecting to my shamanic gifts and power in this lifetime. It was important for me to honour and respect the First Nations people while at the same time honouring myself and the medicine and wisdom that was coming through. I fully respect and honour all that came before me and Indigenous sacred teachings, and have learned that my wounding shouldn't stop me or anyone from connecting to this powerful land and its medicine or with each other. Stepping into my shamanic power had nothing to do with cultural wounding and everything to do with my own empowerment and birthright to work with my personal shamanic gifts.

We are all sacred to the land: we were before, we are now and we will be forever, and I didn't need permission to activate my personal connection with the earth. I realised with a deep knowing that we are all connected and come from the same source, and all of us have the right to connect deeply with our own shamanic practices and the sacred land as long as we respect her and walk kindly, softly, gently and with deep love in our heart. We need to honour and respect the old ways, traditions and ancestors as well as honour our own creation and new ways. This was a huge catalyst in my life, and after integrating this experience I started to birth my workshops around crystal shamanism and the teachings I offer in this book.

I realised over the next few years during other, similar experiences that my shamanic roots ran deep. My heritage goes back to the Celts and my ancestors would have been deeply connected to their shamanic gifts and sacred land; the shamanic connection is in my DNA. Every one of us has innate knowing and connection to our shamanic roots at their core. Most of us have been disconnected and so far removed from our culture, ancestors and their ways, but our ancestors are still with us in spirit and helping us from beyond the veils of the spirit world. Stepping into your power as a medicine person and connecting deeply to the medicine of the land has nothing to do with colour or race and it does not discriminate. We all come from and go back to the same source of all that is; we are all one at the source, one love and one tribe. There is a deep wound of not belonging and many of us have wandered far from the shamanic way and natural connection to earth, but it's time to deeply reconnect for yourself

and the planet and know that this connection has always been there waiting for you to awaken and remember, and to know that you are never alone and that your ancestors have never left you. They are always guiding us all from the spirit world.

CRYSTAL ALLY

RED JASPER

All types of crystals will assist in holding space for sacred ceremonies. Crystals come from the earth and amplify your intention, so you need to connect into your heart and ask which crystal would like to assist you in your ceremony. Decide what your ceremony is about and choose a crystal that aligns with your intention. The most common crystals utilised in ceremonies by native peoples of the world are red jasper, bustamite, opal and phenacite. Native Americans worked with clear quartz with the intention to deepen their connection to the earth. Red jasper is a stone of nurturing and grounding, and it:

- is used in ceremonies and rituals for protection

- connects you to Mother Earth and draws her healing energy up into the body, creating strength and balance

- connects you with your ancestors

- assists you in setting healthy boundaries

- awakens ancient memories

- helps you overcome any deep-seated fear of abandonment

- enables you to let go of controlling behaviours.

Me birthing a sacred medicine drum.

Gog in Glastonbury.

Magog in Glastonbury.

The man from Sedona who
gifted me the heart stone.

Me in sacred circle
in Sedona.

Sacred ceremony.

Sacred medicine wheel
in Sedona.

Sacred altar.

Me in the petrified wood forest.

Seth, the sacred snake.

Me and Dad.

Jeremy Donovan at the Sacred Journey Within retreat.

Machu Picchu in Peru.

Sacred site in the sacred valley in Peru.

With Edwin in Choquequirao in Peru doing a condor ceremony.

Lost city of the Incas, Machu Picchu, in Choquequirao in Peru.

Edwin.

Machu Picchu, Peru.

Me after a five-day hike to Machu Picchu.

A Spanish lady and me at a sacred site in Peru.

The Sacred Journey Within retreat.

Edwin and me in Cusco, Peru, undertaking ceremony.

Birthing my first drum.

Me on sacred journey.

YOUR CEREMONY

You can create whatever ceremony you would like; for example, healing, manifesting, deeper connection to spirit or honouring your ancestors just to name a few. Decide what you would like to do your ceremony for and build your process around your intention.

To give you some ideas and to make it easier for you I offer you a letting-go ceremony. For this ceremony you will need sage or incense, a favourite cleansed crystal and a drum or rattle. To begin, acknowledge the Traditional Custodians of the land on which you stand and pay your respects to their Elders past and present and future generations. Then:

- Smudge yourself and your sacred space with the intention of clearing any unwanted energy.
- Close your eyes and take some time to call in your medicine and spirit helpers: the spirits of the land, spirit guides, angels, your ancestors, Mother Earth, Father Sky, the elements, animal guides, crystal devas, light beings, gods and goddesses, the directions, your higher self and anyone else you connect with.
- Set the intention for help to let go of any stuck and stale energy that may be holding you back from being the best possible version of yourself.
- Take a moment to gather up into a ball at your heart any energy that is held in your body, mind or spirit that is not of your highest good, then place your crystal on your heart and send this energy into your crystal.
- Hold the crystal up to your mouth, blow the energy up to the sky and ask that the energy gets transmitted back to love.
- Spend time playing your drum or rattle or dance to let go of any remaining stale energy. Stop when you feel the energy has been dispersed.
- Send love and blessings to all of the beings that assisted in your ceremony.

Record your experience.

_____
_____
_____
_____
_____
_____
_____
_____
_____
_____
_____
_____
_____
_____
_____
_____
_____
_____
_____
_____
_____

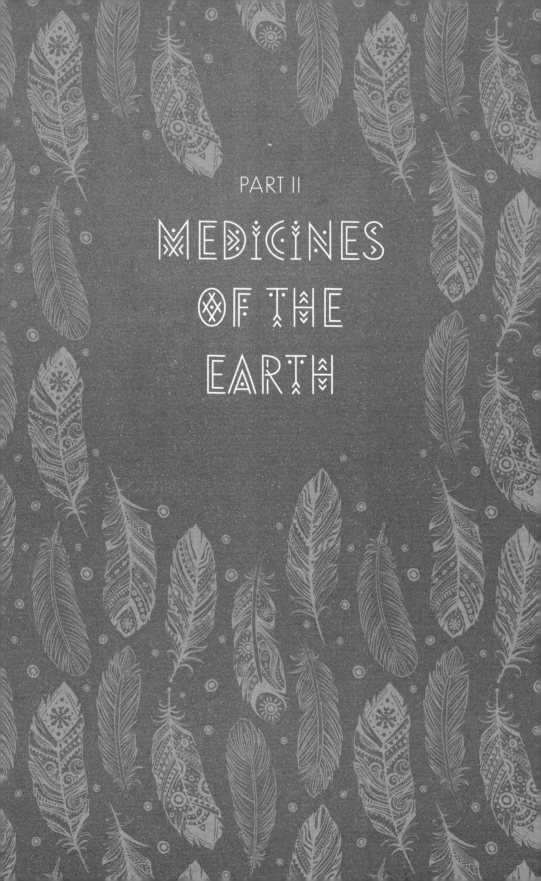

PART II

MEDICINES OF THE EARTH

'Medicines of the earth' references everything that is alive within nature and exists on this earthly plane: trees, elements, animals, crystals and the sun, moon and stars. We co-create with an abundance of different animals, plants and living beings, and each one has a soul and spirit. There is an energetic connection between everything that exists within nature and this world, from the inner realms of the earth and far out into the stars and different galaxies.

Everything that is alive has an energy frequency and specific medicine to share with us. As we build a strong relationship to the living things of the earth we are then able to receive the medicine and energy they have to offer. This union is truly sacred and has been understood by ancient peoples for thousands of years. It's important to know that your actions can affect the energies of all living things and your relationship with them, so it's vital to respect, protect and honour this union on every level.

The medicines of the earth are also within you, and when you connect with their energy this medicine is activated in you and gives you an opportunity to heal, align and balance yourself. As you create a relationship with the spirit of earth energies you align with the medicine and healing energy that is within you. I hope that by sharing my stories and understanding of the powerful earth medicines and introducing you to their healing spirits you will be able to build your own personal relationship with them and create a deeper connection.

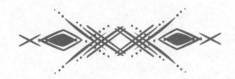

CHAPTER 3

CRYSTALS

Crystals are sacred gifts from the earth that have been utilised for thousands of years and understood for their transformational healing powers and magical wisdom by indigenous and tribal people worldwide. The Aboriginal people of Australia connected to crystals to assist them in accessing the Dreamtime. The Egyptians ground down crystals and used them as make-up for spiritual initiations, and buried them with mummies to protect the dead in the afterlife. The famous crystal skulls found in the Mayan temples in Mexico shared wisdom and knowledge about life with tribal people, while Native Americans utilised crystals to amplify their connection and communication to the land in ceremonies.

Crystals are ubiquitous in modern society, with computer and internet systems being run by crystal technology. There are crystals in our watches to keep the time and in our computers to store information. Modern-day science has come to realise that crystals are not just pretty rocks and is truly starting to understand their powers. Crystals are not as airy-fairy as you might think they are, as science has proven that crystals store energy and

work within the laws of physics. Crystals are alive and have a consciousness of their own.

THE MEDICINE OF CRYSTALS

Each crystal has its own specific vibration or medicine and radiates divine love and pure energy from Mother Earth and the universe, and when you are in the presence of a crystal it amplifies the medicine inside you and invokes an innate intelligence of self-healing, giving you an opportunity for transformation. In the process of self-healing your emotional, mental, spiritual and physical bodies attain balance. Crystals encourage and assist you to live in the now so you can start to truly understand that we are all connected to the universe at all times. They remind you of your true essence of oneness and connection to source. Crystals shine a light into hidden parts of you that may have been forgotten over time, and invite you to transform old energy to create balance and well-being.

Everything in the universe is made up of energy and vibration and is connected to the one source of universal energy, which is explained in a science known as sacred geometry. There are five main shapes, or blueprints, that energy organises and aligns itself to as it manifests into a physical form. All life on the planet stems from these shapes, called the five platonic solids. Crystals are pure energy made up of atoms, and the atoms are the inner structure of energy. Crystals are formed and birthed when the atoms of energy align to the platonic solids, a process that allows each crystal to be unique: holding different energy, colour and vibration. Everything on the physical plane is created from these energetic structures, all vibrating at different frequencies with different combinations of atoms aligning through the five platonic solids and sacred geometry.

The sacred relationship between the crystal kingdom and living beings allows for deep transformation and healing to occur on many levels. The similarities between crystals and the human body allow the cells of the body to communicate with each other, creating a transfer of energy and allowing the innate intelligence of the body to heal itself. Crystal healing is actually a science and works within a law of physics – the law of resonance – which states that 'like energy attracts like energy'. This is why when we

are in the presence of crystals they assist us in aligning with the healing energy within.

Throughout your life you will experience many challenges that you sometimes misinterpret, which then creates pain, hurt and fear, and you may tend to shut off from yourself and those around you. This process creates suppressed emotions within your energy field that can lie dormant, creating unwanted behavioural patterns in your life. The resulting imbalance in your energy body can eventually create disease within the physical body, as suppressed emotions and old patterns and belief systems are stored in your energy fields and become emotional baggage. This may in turn lead you to feel as though you are not whole, and the illusion of separation from source starts to take place as you begin to identify yourself as your issues instead of your true essence and divinity.

Crystals create a safe, sacred space to discard the old, suppressed emotions and unwanted patterns from your fields. Crystals know they are pure love and light of the universe and assist you to connect with your higher self, with your pure essence, as you align to the love and order of the universe, allowing transformation and deep healing to occur. Crystal vibrations resonate with the energy in the body and the auric field, and any imbalances rise as memories of the past. As you are held in the vibration of love and truth and with your heart open you are able to expand your awareness to see the truth within these experiences and are given an opportunity to accept and release the issues. You then move out of the old way of being and open to receive the blessings and gifts from this experience. You can surrender yourself and be free of the chains of your old perception as you move deeper into your heart and accept, love and nurture all aspects of yourself. This process creates a deep connection between your heart and soul and an opportunity to look deeply into your inner self with unconditional love and trust.

From my own experiences of healing I have come to understand that our most powerful gifts are hidden beneath our fears, in those places we feel uncomfortable. This place, which is commonly called the shadow, is where your power lies and your true gifts are. There is always a blessing offered with a challenge; you just have to have the courage to look for it. This is a sacred process of healing, and when truly understood and felt in

the heart it allows for personal growth, an expanded awareness of self and deep transformation and awakening. It creates deep gratitude for life and allows us to know and accept ourselves completely. The healing journey makes you who you are and creates great strength and courage of spirit.

MY PERSONAL EXPERIENCE

I have had an abundance of experiences with crystals. The most profound and life changing was my first: it was my crystal awakening and it dramatically changed the direction of my life in a positive way. There is so much to this awakening; however, for now I will try to give you the core of what happened for me.

For a great part of my life I felt lost in a world of darkness and inner pain, as though I was searching for something. I experienced serious depression and anxiety and turned to addictions to soothe my emotional turmoil. I was walking asleep and had no idea who I was or what my purpose was meant to be or how I was going to get out of it, until I finally hit rock bottom. Around the year 2000 there was a huge energy shift on the planet and a downloading of Christ consciousness that initiated my awakening and expanded awareness. The life I knew was rapidly changing.

A friend gifted me my first crystal, but back then I thought they were just pretty rocks. I found out pretty quickly that they are sacred medicine here to assist humanity in its healing and awakening. My first crystal experience blew me off the planet, bringing light to the deepest part of my soul and waking me from my unconscious sleep. One evening I sat with the amethyst crystal my friend had given me along with a clear quartz crystal I had purchased, and it was as though a lightning bolt had exploded from within me and permeated throughout every cell of my being. My body started to shake and my breathing became laboured, and I was frightened and told myself to breathe, just breathe. I entered into a deep state of trance and went on a huge spiritual and soul awakening, and for three days and three nights I didn't eat or sleep.

I realised that I had placed myself in a box that was made up of beliefs I had taken on from my parents, teachers, friends and life itself about who I needed to be so I would be loved and respected. I had lived my

life thinking I was this box; however, in my awakening I realised I was not the box, that I was not my beliefs or my emotions, and I arrived at a big question: if I'm not who I thought I was then who was I? Then came a deep understanding that we are all connected to something extremely powerful: a greater power, a divine presence.

I felt peace and bliss for the first time in my life and was deeply connected with the energy of divine love. I spent days in this healing energy uncovering wounds I held in my psyche and emotions that had been stuck in my body that I had been holding on to from the challenging experiences and trauma I had had in my life. As these wounds showed themselves and emotions came to the surface I could see things in a different light, I could see for the first time the blessings that were offered in such pain and challenge. It was as though I was reviewing my life, and as I had a memory of each trauma I could feel love for myself and see this experience in a more expanded awareness and understanding. I could see why my soul had chosen to have these uncomfortable experiences: so I could gain the profound lessons and gifts I subsequently received, gifts of strength, courage, empathy and deep passion and drive to help others.

The crystal medicine and profound experience of self-love, forgiveness and compassion allowed me to connect to the love of my soul and see the higher truth in my life. I was able to let go of the stale energy that had been held in my being, and the shift in my consciousness woke up my soul as I birthed the wisdom of crystal healing into my world.

After this experience I found my crystal healing teacher, Maggie Vrinda Ross, and was nurtured and guided down a new path that sparked a passion for crystals and a drive to continue delving into healing. After many other profound and amazing experiences I created the Academy of Crystal Awakening, in which I have mentored more than 10,000 people and trained more than 50 teachers to share the love and healing from the crystal kingdom. The academy ran from 2000 to 2021 and I offered two separate healing modalities: Rachelle Charman's Crystal Awakening and Rachelle Charman's Crystal Shamanism. The academy became an approved training provider with the International Institute for Complementary Therapists, and both modalities became recognised and approved and are still taught by myself and others to this day.

YOUR PERSONAL CRYSTAL HEALING

For a personal crystal healing ceremony, intuitively choose three crystals you would like to receive a healing from, always working with crystals that have been cleansed and charged. Make sure you are well hydrated, then:

◈ Prepare your healing space and clear any unwanted energies in the room by burning sage.

◈ Call upon your healing guides, angels and crystal devas. When you step into a sacred healing space you become a channel for healing energy, which is why it is important to call upon helpers from the spirit world to guide your way.

◈ Set the healing space by saying an invocation that allows you to open to divine healing energy from the universe (see opposite). Feel free to use your own invocation if you have one.

◈ Set the intention that this healing is for the highest good of all.

◈ Close your eyes and focus on your breath as you drop into a state of deep relaxation.

◈ Visualise golden light streaming down from the universe through your crown chakra and into your heart, and direct this energy into and offer it to the earth.

◈ Draw up healing energy from the earth, then expand these two energies of love within your heart.

◈ Place one crystal on your heart and call in the deva to shower you with the medicine.

◈ For one minute take long, deep breaths: on each inhale draw in the energy of the crystal to your heart and on the exhale send love to the crystal.

◈ For the second minute take long, deep breaths: on the inhale draw in the energy of the crystal to your heart and on the exhale send the energy of the crystal into your body and all of your cells.

◈ For the third minute, place the crystal intuitively on your body and open to receive its healing energy. Leave the crystal there until you feel the energy subside.

- Repeat the process with the other two crystals.
- Thank the crystal devas.

Healing invocation

> *I invoke the love of the divine universe within my heart.*
> *I am a clear and pure channel.*
> *Love is my guide.*
>
> *I invoke the love of the divine universe within my heart.*
> *I am a clear and pure channel.*
> *Love is my guide.*
>
> *I invoke the love of the divine universe within my heart.*
> *I am a clear and pure channel.*
> *Love is my guide.*
>
> *And I follow that love.*

Record your experience.

_____

_____

_____

_____

_____

_____

_____

PRACTITIONER CRYSTAL HEALING

Connect with your client and discuss what they would like healing for. Depending on what your client's intention is, intuitively choose three crystals that align with the intention, always working with crystals that have been cleansed and charged. Make sure you are well hydrated, then:

- Prepare the healing space and clear any unwanted energies in the room by burning sage.

- Take a few moments to connect with your crystals and yourself.

- Call upon your healing guides, angels and crystal devas. When you step into a sacred healing space you become a channel for healing energy, which is why it is important to call upon helpers from the spirit world to guide your way.

- Set the healing space by saying an invocation that allows you to open to divine healing energy from the universe (see opposite). Feel free to use your own invocation.

- Set the intention that this healing is for the highest good of all.

- Ask your client to close their eyes and focus on their breath as they move deeply into a state of relaxation.

- Visualise golden light streaming down from the universe through your crown chakra and into your heart, then direct this energy into and offer it to the earth. Expand the energy of love within your heart and down your arms and hands. This will open your heart so you can share the energy in the healing.

- Place one crystal on your client's heart, and guide them on a breathing/ connecting process of drawing the crystal energy into their heart on their in breath and sending love to the crystal on their out breath. Do this for one minute and make sure they breathe deeply; the longer and deeper they breathe the more light they will bring in.

- The next minute guide them to draw the crystal medicine in on the in breath, and on the out breath guide them to burst the crystal light into and around their body.

* Place the crystal on the person's body where you intuitively feel they require energy the most, and send love to the crystal and guide the energy into your client's cells. The crystal has an innate intelligence of its own and knows what to do and where to go, and your intention will amplify this process.

* Once the crystal has done its work you will feel the energy subside.

* Repeat the process with the other two crystals.

* Guide your client gently back into the room by saying:

> '*I call all aspects of the self back into the room, into the physical. When you're ready, slowly open your eyes.*'

You may also choose words of your own.

Ask your client to share their experience and take the time to listen to and support them with an open heart in unconditional love. Share with your client any messages you received from the universe, spirit or crystal devas in the healing.

Healing invocation

> *I invoke the love of the divine universe within my heart.*
> *I am a clear and pure channel.*
> *Love is my guide.*
> *I invoke the love of the divine universe within my heart.*
> *I am a clear and pure channel.*
> *Love is my guide.*
> *I invoke the love of the divine universe within my heart.*
> *I am a clear and pure channel.*
> *Love is my guide.*
> *And I follow that love.*

CHAPTER 4

POWER ANIMALS AND TOTEM ANIMALS OR ALLIES

Everyone has a main power animal that guides them through their life, similar to a spirit guide or guardian angel. We also have other animals that come in at different times as allies to share their medicine and guidance when needed. Many ancient cultures had connections with and beliefs around animal totems, believing that animals guided them and offered different wisdom, protection, support, friendship and healing energy when required. Although the details may have differed from tribe to tribe, the main understanding that we all are deeply connected to the spirit of these animals is the same.

THE MEDICINE OF ANIMALS

Each animal has its own unique medicine and shows up in your life when you need this specific guidance or healing. As you become aware of their presence and connect deeply with this energy, it will help you to trigger and connect with this same energy within you. It helps you to align with and empower a vibration you already have inside you, just as crystals amplify the light within you.

Each person has their own unique connection and relationship with their animal totem or animal spirit guide. There is myriad information on the internet and in books about what a particular animal's energy offers; however, the most important way to understand the medicine is by building and deepening a personal relationship with the animal spirit. Another way to understand the medicine is by witnessing the behaviour of the animal in its natural habitat. For example, a bear forages for herbs and healing plants before hibernating during winter. The medicine of the bear, known as the healer of the animal kingdom, is very much about this energy. Usually, how an animal exists in its natural environment and the gifts it has will mirror the medicine it has in the spirit world.

Power animals

Everyone has a main spirit helper, known as a power animal, that assists in integrating this specific medicine and its unique traits throughout their life's journey. There is a soul contract with the animal spirit before you come into the earth plane. Your power animal will stay with you for your complete life

experience, from birth to death, and is always by your side. When you start to become aware of your spirit animals it can sometimes be difficult to know for sure which one is your actual power animal. My advice would be to not get too fixated on whether they are your power animal or not, rather to work with the energy and medicine they are sharing. Many different animals will come and go, but if there is one that stays and is always present there's a strong possibility it is your main power animal.

Totem animals or allies

Similar to your power animal you have other animal spirit guides, known as totem animals or allies, that will come into your life at the perfect time to offer specific energy and will remain with you on your journey until you have integrated this medicine into your life. They assist you in learning or integrating the unique traits or energies of their spirit and come and go depending upon what medicine, guidance and support is required. Some ancient tribes also believe that you have a family spirit totem that offers guidance, support and wisdom to the collective energy of the tribe.

Connecting with your animal guides

There are several different ways to connect with and become aware of your animal spirit totems, including:

- ❧ *Physically*: your animal guide can come to you in a physical form by crossing your path so you actually see them in your space, or you may notice them over and over in repetition on the TV or internet or in conversation. They start showing up everywhere to get your attention.

- ❧ *Dream state*: you may receive animal totems and allies while you are in a dream state. They come to offer healing and guidance while you sleep.

⋘ *Spiritually*: one way that has been used for centuries is to meet animal guides in the inner realms and trance-like states. Your spirit animal resides within the inner realms and you can travel there to receive their healing and medicine. Once you know what your power animal is they become your guide in the three shamanic worlds (see Part IV).

Although I connect with my animal guides through various means, most of my animal experiences happen in the physical world. I believe this is because I am very grounded and earth based. When I trance travel into either of the three shamanic worlds I ask the ally for confirmation outside this space and ask them to show up three times in the physical world. I do this so I feel confident in what I have received, which is a great way of building trust and allows me to connect with the medicine on a deeper level.

MY PERSONAL EXPERIENCE

We each have our own special connections to the wonderful animal kingdom and our animal guides, and I hope my personal stories invoke your very own special stories and memories. Opportunities to connect with the animal kingdom happen constantly, and you will clearly see the signs and confirmations and receive the deep medicine and wisdom of animals as you become more aware of what is happening around you.

Snake medicine

My connection with and deeper understanding of animal totems started when I moved out of the city to live in the country: from Bondi in Sydney to a 20-hectare property in a deep valley in northern New South Wales, 40 minutes from any shops and surrounded by nature. Three weeks after I moved there snakes started showing up, and their energy was electrifying and I could feel the medicine permeating every cell of my being. The snakes were certainly getting my attention: I constantly found snake skins lying around and saw at least two or three snakes a day.

I quickly found out I had a deep fear of snakes. I was petrified every night before I went to sleep and checked under the sheets and bed and in

the cupboards and closed all the doors so I was safely tucked away from what I thought at the time were dangerous creatures. The fear was so bad I was constantly on edge, and anything that slightly represented a cord or stick looked like a snake that was out to get me. I even wondered at one point how I could get out of my lease, for my beautiful sanctuary had quickly turned into a place I was petrified to be in.

After accepting there was no way out and that I was stuck with having snakes as housemates I thought it was time to tune in to why I was so scared, and I realised I thought the snakes were going to kill me and I was scared of death. I started to connect with the snakes on a whole new level, assuring myself they were not trying to scare or kill me, and I had a deep knowing that they were there to teach me. The fear started to subside with each day as I connected more and more deeply with this powerful medicine.

I had one favourite snake named Seth, who slept outside my bedroom window, and every morning when I woke my first thought was that I hoped Seth was still there. I looked out the window to make sure he was. It was a big turnaround from wanting them all gone to feeling comforted by their presence. Seth became by best friend, at times communicating telepathically with me. I shared many meditations with him and the other snakes that lived inside the walls of my home. They shared with me that there was no reason to be scared of death, that in one form or another something is dying in each moment. Cells and organs are constantly shedding and rebuilding themselves in the physical body, and emotionally and mentally we are letting go of old beliefs and stale emotions much like snakes shed their skins.

As I spent time with these powerful and sacred creatures I came to understand the snake medicine deeply. I was able to tune in to and see what they were showing and teaching me. I ended up feeling deeply touched and grateful for such an experience, and once I fully received the gift the snakes moved on and I never saw them again. I had fully embodied their medicine of transformation and looking at death in a sacred light within me.

Eagle medicine

This powerful story is very close and dear to my heart, as it highlights the potent medicine of animal guides, past lives and soul retrieval and that the shamanic way and this healing wisdom is definitely real and tangible.

Many years ago while I was living in the city I attended my first-ever drumming circle. As I stood in the centre of about 30 people drumming I had a profound healing experience: I was greeted by my power animal for the first time. This huge, loving, protective brown bear guided me up to a mountaintop, and I saw myself inside a medicine circle as a young Native American boy. I shouted out to spirit in disbelief and grief: 'You took my father.' I felt intense pain in my body and realised I had brought this energy into my current lifetime. I had the knowing that someone had killed my father, who was the chief of the tribe, and was angry at spirit for allowing this to happen.

I then realised that the chief in this vision was also my dad in this lifetime. One of my biggest traumas in this life was when my father left our family when I was about eight years old. It was my first heartbreak and created deep wounds around the masculine that have been a work in progress and a labour of love to heal. As I came out of my trance-like state and visualisation I had a huge 'Aha' moment: I realised I had been eight years old in the vision, the same age as when my dad had left me in this current life. I had spent most of my life blaming myself for him leaving and had constant thoughts that I wasn't enough and worthy of love; however, when I understood my dad had left me in the past life at the same age I had a deep realisation that it wasn't my fault he had left, that it was a karmic playout and opportunity to heal this old wound that I had also brought into this life once and for all.

The experience had cycled itself so I could deal with the pain and finally heal from this deep wound and set myself free from the old energy and emotions. It was the start of a very deep healing journey that had carried over many lifetimes. Over the next few years I did everything I could to connect with my father without success: he constantly rejected me due to his own pain and shame until one day I decided to pull away and not push myself into his life any more as it was too painful. I had

to set some healthy boundaries for myself and start to look after my emotional well-being.

Years went by during which I had nothing to do with my dad, when one day out of the blue I received the dreaded phone call: his wife had called to let me know he had severe lung cancer and I knew in my heart that he didn't have much time left to live. He had decided to undergo a course of chemotherapy, and his wife was caring for him at home. I flew to Sydney with my brother to visit him, but it was incredibly sad as he felt like a stranger to me. I left with a heavy feeling in my heart and with the realisation that I might not ever see him again.

I couldn't live with this feeling and decided to go to see him once more, but he had badly deteriorated and was permanently laid up in bed. As I sat with him I wondered what I should say to this man, my father, who felt like a stranger yet with whom I had a deep heart connection. He was going in and out of sleep, and I put my hand on him and said: 'Just rest, Dad, just rest,' as I sat with him in this sacred space.

I closed my eyes and dropped into a state of deep relaxation. I then had a vision, the same past-life vision of myself as the young Native American boy on the mountaintop screaming in pain. However, there was something different about this vision, because this time there was an eagle in the sky that offered me a sense of comfort from my pain. The eagle in Native American tradition represents our connection with the father, Father Sky.

I sat with my dad in this space for hours before I reluctantly decided it was time to go. As I walked from his room I said to him: 'I will never see you again,' and he replied, 'Yes, you will.' It was one of the hardest moments of my life, but what happened next was amazing and deeply touched my heart and soul on every level. I got in my car and started to drive down the street, and guess what I saw? Yes: an eagle in the sky! It blew me away but I felt so comforted by its presence, as though it was supporting me. After that I saw at least one eagle every day; they were watching over me and helping me deal with the pain of my father's pending death and the grief I had held on to for many lifetimes.

A few months passed and I had a strong sense to pick up my guitar and write my father a song, as I had struggled to talk with him for many years

and still had unspoken words to share. As I sat down to play I looked out of the window, and once again the eagles were there guiding and supporting me. They were circling my house and I feel they gifted me a song to sing to my father. The song, which I called 'Fly Like an Eagle', was all about him going home on eagles' wings and how much I forgave and loved him.

Fly Like an Eagle

> *Your spirit is alive and you're going home*
> *Soar like an eagle, free your soul.*
> *Thank you for the healing; you make my spirit whole*
> *I will see you again sometime, you're never alone.*
>
> *Soar like an eagle*
> *Flying home.*
> *Fly with the angels*
> *Free your soul.*
> *Fly high on eagles' wings*
> *Fly your spirit high, on angels' wings.*
>
> *You bring us love, you bring us strength*
> *You bring us light, you bring it all.*
>
> *You touched so many people in this life, you know*
> *Sharing your heart with the people you know.*
> *You will always be remembered for your warm and loving glow*
> *And now it's time to fly and let your spirit flow.*

Days went by before I gathered up the courage to send this song to my father; I was scared of the possibility of being rejected again and thought the song might upset him. I was feeling a little stressed, so I decided to take my beautiful pup Gaia down to the beach for a walk to clear my head. As I drove down the street I saw three eagles sitting in a tree, so I drove home and dragged my partner outside to witness what I had seen as

I couldn't believe my eyes. My agreement with spirit is that when I see things in threes it is a strong confirmation of truth, and seeing those three eagles was a confirmation for me to send the song to my dad. I grabbed my phone and sent a recording of the song to him.

I never heard or spoke to him after that, but a few days later my stepbrother called to say that my dad had passed over. I later found out after talking to my stepmother that Dad had listened to the song over and over and wept as he passed into the spirit world. I felt truly blessed to have shared such precious, truly sacred and powerful medicine with my father through this song, and I believe it set him free. I grieved over my dad's passing but it greatly healed my heart. I realised I had been grieving for him for lifetimes, but as my dad was finally set free so was my pain. He could no longer reject me, and it started my connection with him from the spirit world.

After some time I had an awareness that my lifetime as the Native American boy was in Sedona, Arizona and I had a strong pull and calling to go there for my 40th birthday. I wasn't sure how I would get there, but I left it to spirit to come through and they certainly did. For years I had been collecting the names of people who wanted to buy a rare crystal, and that week a crystal wholesaler called me to ask if I knew anyone who wanted to buy this specific crystal. I was able to on-sell some and make the money I needed to go to Sedona. I realised that the Tucson gem festival was going to be on at the same time and had a sense that the crystal kingdom had paid for me to go on this journey.

On my arrival in Sedona I met a beautiful man and powerful shaman named Clay. He didn't know my story or why I was there, but he was a deeply connected man and I had a sense that we had been fated to meet. He drove me up into the mountains, and I found myself in the middle of a medicine circle on top of a mountain. It was the same mountain I had seen in my vision with my dad in my Native American life, and it was absolutely incredible that I found myself physically in the same place lifetimes apart.

Clay told me to let it out, to let it go and shout it out. I could feel the pain rising from deep within my being and was finally able to scream out and release the pain I had been holding for lifetimes. Releasing this pain

meant I was also able to retrieve the part of my soul I had left in this time and place from the past life. I was on this mountain retrieving a part of my heart, and as this was happening there he was: a huge eagle looking down at me from high in the sky that I know was my dad's spirit. You can't make this stuff up! It was a hugely profound and tangible healing for me on many levels.

The story continues: while I was in Sedona I met another shaman who also took me out on the land and offered me healing and a powerful shamanic process. I was asked to lie down on the land and close my eyes while he drummed a trance beat over me. He said there was someone waiting in a cave for me, then he guided me to see myself walking over red rocks and into a cave. I waited a while and then the vision came strong and clear: my dad was there in a Native American headdress and he welcomed me and bent down to scoop up some red dirt. The sand fell through his fingers, and what was left was a red rock in the shape of a heart made from the earth. He gifted me this rock and guided me to put it in my heart. I had returned to Sedona to retrieve a piece of my heart, and this experience was another confirmation that it was actually happening.

The next day I hiked up one of the many sacred mountains in Sedona, and on my way down I ran into a man who was the spitting image of my father. I was astounded, and I stopped him and asked if we could have a photo taken together and he agreed. I asked a lady who was walking the same trail if she would take the picture, and as she took the camera from me the man reached into his pocket and pulled out a red rock in the shape of a heart. He gifted it to me, and I was so shocked it didn't register straight away what had happened. After a while it started to sink in: it was the same heart-shaped rock my father had given me in the vision. Wow: what a powerful confirmation that my heart was finally healed from the grief, pain, loss and rejection!

Shamans say that when you receive a gift in the spirit world and it shows up in the physical world you are ready to work with it or it is a strong sign of profound healing. This story truly highlights the power of past-life, soul retrieval and crystal medicine and how they are tangible medicine spirits to connect and work with for deep soul healing.

CRYSTAL ALLY

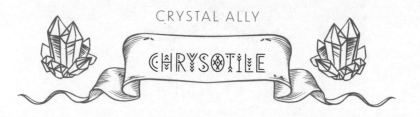

CHRYSOTILE

Chrysotile, the crystal I share in my story about shapeshifting into a spider later in the book, acts as a powerful ally to connect with and awaken you to animal spirit guides. It was gifted to me as I was deepening my understanding of animal medicine and I went on to have many personal experiences. This crystal was a powerful ally and guide for me in truly understanding animal medicine and how it can help us on our journey through life. Chrysotile:

⟪ allows you to connect deeply with your power animal in spirit

⟪ allows deep connection to the inner worlds

⟪ assists your awakening to the wisdom of the animal kingdom and what it has to share.

YOUR CEREMONY

Carry out this ceremony if you wish to connect with an animal spirit:

- ⧎ Take some time out of your schedule to sit quietly and connect.
- ⧎ Set an intention that you would like to receive wisdom or healing regarding something in your life.
- ⧎ Call upon an animal spirit to show up in your life to offer you its medicine.
- ⧎ Offer a gift back to the spirit such as a song, drumming, rattle, dance, poem or a prayer of love. Whenever you ask something from the spirit world it is important to honour the process and the spirit by offering energy back. This can be in any form you choose.

After this ceremony, make sure you are aware and take notice when the medicine shows up in your life as it's important to honour the sacred medicine by receiving it when it arrives.

Record your experience.

_____

_____

_____

_____

_____

_____

_____

_____

CHAPTER 5

TREES

Just like all the other earthly beings have medicine to share with us, so too do trees.

THE MEDICINE OF TREES

Each tree has a specific energy and medicine to share, and when we take the time to connect deeply we are able to receive their energy. For centuries the medicine men and women of many cultures have honoured, understood and worked with tree medicine and the sacred connection and relationship with them, a relationship that runs deep. We would not be able to live on this planet without trees: along with plants they are the lungs of the planet, removing carbon dioxide and other toxins from the atmosphere and producing the oxygen we breathe.

Their roots extend deep down into the earth and their branches reach up to the heavens, allowing them to be powerful conductors of energy of the two mediums of heaven and earth. They are the portal on the physical

plane for entering into the three worlds of shamanism that medicine men and women travel to in order to receive energy and medicine for healing. You can enter energetically in a trance state or via meditation through a hole in the trunk of a tree, and travel to the upper, middle or lower realm (see Part IV). Trees also hold the wisdom and knowledge of the ancestors, and when someone passes their body returns to the earth and their wisdom is held within the roots of the trees that extend down to the inner realms.

MY PERSONAL EXPERIENCE

Me connecting with Magog.

Who doesn't love a good tree hug! I've had several powerful moments with trees, which has shown me without a doubt they are alive and have a spirit or soul. We wouldn't be able to live on this planet if it wasn't for our co-existence with trees, and the connection definitely runs deep. I have been

blessed to have travelled to some very sacred places and met with potent ancient trees, for instance Gog and Magog, two oak trees that stand as the guardians to the sacred Druid ceremonial grounds in Glastonbury in England. These trees are more than 2,000 years old, and to sit with them and connect with their energy was certainly an honour and true blessing. I felt a deep sense of awe but also of peace in their presence.

Another fantastic experience occurred when I visited the Petrified Forest National Park in Sedona in Arizona. This land was once lush rainforest but the trees, which are thought to be more than 225 million years old, have petrified over time and now lie on the desert floor. As I was walking through this sacred land I had a sense that the trees held the memories and wisdom of many, many years, and I had a deep knowing that no one owns this earth, that we are all her guardians and we need to look after her and treat her as sacred. The trees shared with me that our life is but a drop in the ocean and we shouldn't get caught up with little things in our world, that situations come and go and will finally pass in time. Our ultimate goal is to be as present as we can in the moment and not let our minds and emotions run away from us; to be solid like the trees with our roots grounded in the earth and our branches flowing in the wind; and to learn to be a little more centred and still while at the same time going with the flow of life.

I would love to share another story about one of the most powerful connections I have had with the tree spirits. After years of searching for my ancestors from a past life I started to feel a calling to connect with my blood ancestors. I was invited to my first Celtic circle on a night when the veil between the worlds was at its thinnest and you could connect deeply with your ancestors. As soon as I entered into the sacred circle I felt my ancestors gathering around me, and I could sense a deep essence of love and support.

I realised during this ceremony that my shamanic roots ran back through my own family line but that over hundreds of years our family had forgotten them, just as do most of us in this world. Many of us are so far removed from our cultures and traditions that we have become lost on many levels. We yearn to know where we came from and to feel as though we belong. In the Celtic circle the deep connection I felt in spirit

with my blood ancestors and my roots gave me a deep sense of belonging, that I did come from somewhere. Even though I had never before felt this blood connection in my life, my ancestors were present in spirit guiding and supporting me and were waiting for me to connect with them when I was ready.

I now realise it's a common practice for our ancestors to pray for seven generations up and down the family line. I was being protected and cared for by the prayers of seven generations that had transcended time and space. I knew there had been other medicine people in my family back down through the generations, and later at my dad's funeral his brother shared with me the fact that their grandmother from five generations previously had been a medicine woman.

After my experience in the powerful Celtic circle with my ancestors all I wanted to do was sit with a tree that was calling me in the backyard of my friend's home in Brisbane. I spent days connecting to this spirit and realised I could hear the whispers of my ancestors through the tree. I understood that when our ancestors pass from this world their bodies go back into the land, and the earth retains their memories and wisdom.

Tree roots are embedded deeply in the earth and hold memories and wisdom, so when we connect with trees we are connecting with those memories and the energy of our ancestors. It was a huge 'Aha' moment for me and I sat for days communing and being taught by my kin. Celtic people believe we have a power tree that guides us in our current lifetime, just as we have a power animal.

The time I spent in Glastonbury also sparked my awareness and passion to connect deeply with the medicine of trees, and I was naturally drawn to Druid tree books to help me understand this knowledge. It was the start of my awakening to tree medicine, and this wisdom runs deep within my DNA. My ancestors had shared with me that shamanic wisdom is in my blood and bones and urged me to continue looking within for the answers. All of us have shamanic roots from our ancestry, and this wisdom of earth medicine runs deep for us all. I invite you to give yourself time to connect deeply with your shamanic roots, becoming aware of what nature and your ancestors are saying to you and being open to receive their medicine. It's your birthright.

CRYSTAL ALLIES

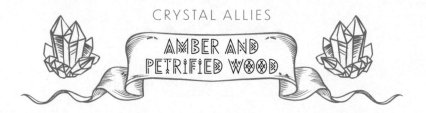

AMBER AND
PETRIFIED WOOD

Some crystals that will assist you to create a deeper connection with trees are amber, the fossilised resin from a tree, and petrified wood.

Amber:

- ⫸ enables you to have a deeper connection with nature and tree spirits
- ⫸ draws disease from your body
- ⫸ assists in dissolving old patterns from the past that are handed down through your DNA
- ⫸ helps to create a deep connection with your ancestors so you can receive their deep life wisdom.

Petrified wood:

- ⫸ is a strong grounding stone and centring crystal
- ⫸ assists in connecting you with tree spirits so you can receive deep wisdom and healing from your ancestors
- ⫸ assists in releasing any ancestral karma that has been brought down through your bloodline
- ⫸ awakens the deep knowledge that lies within the blood and bones of your ancestry.

YOUR CEREMONY

If you wish to connect with a tree, undertake this ceremony. It can be done with any tree; however, it is best to do it with a tree with which you feel connected:

- Sit with your back against your tree or, if that is not physically possible, imagine yourself doing so.
- Send love and gratitude to the tree.
- Start to tune in to and let the tree know you would like to create a connection, allowing a few minutes for the tree to respond.
- Once you get a sense that the spirit of the tree is with you, ask it any questions you have.
- Be open to receiving the wisdom or healing the tree has to offer you.
- Stay in this place for as long as you feel guided to.
- When you are finished, make sure you thank the tree. You might like to offer a piece of your hair or a crystal or song to the tree for sharing its sacred energy.

Record your experience.

_____

_____

_____

_____

_____

_____

_____

_____

CHAPTER 6

PLANTS, FLOWERS AND HERBS

For thousands of years plant, flower and herb medicines have been utilised by tribal and indigenous people worldwide.

THE MEDICINE OF PLANTS, FLOWERS AND HERBS

Just as with crystals, each plant has its own specific vibration, medicine and spirit. Over the years shamans have communicated with plant spirits, which guided them and instructed them on how to use the medicine to offer healing and create deep, long-lasting relationships with it. We still use the healing benefits of plants and herbs in natural medicines, and a large percentage of synthetic medicines are based on plant medicine compounds. There is no sickness in the world that cannot be treated with plant medicine.

There are many different ways to utilise the healing properties of this powerful natural medicine. They are used homeopathically, where their energy is expressed into a water-based solution and ingested; for example, in bush flower and Bach flower essences. Another application is the creation of essential oils, a process of extracting the oil from the plant, flower or herb and utilising its healing properties by burning the oil or applying it to the skin. There is also Chinese herbal medicine, which dates back more than 2,200 years. The Chinese people used sacred herbs to create healing remedies that are still used today.

Plants, flowers and herbs have a spirit or higher consciousness that is sometimes referred to as a 'deva'. You can work with this spirit of plants to deepen your connection and relationship with this medicine and receive healing energy on a deeper level. Many edible herbs also have healing properties, and herbs such as sage and eucalyptus are burned and used as ceremony sacraments for honouring and cleaning sacred space.

Then there is the medicine of the master plants, those with particularly strong curative and spiritual powers such as peyote and ayahuasca, that have been used by indigenous peoples as sacred sacrament, healing tools and to connect directly with the spiritual realms. Most of the master plant medicines offer a psychaedelic or mind-altering experience to enable a connection with cosmic universal energies; many people have spiritual out-of-body experiences that create a catalyst for healing on many levels.

Master plant medicine is becoming very popular in modern-day society for its help in healing addictions, depression, anxiety, PTSD and many other mind-, emotion- and brain-related illnesses. It offers healing to the psyche and tangible, long-lasting, positive change for those who choose to integrate the experiences into their day-to-day reality. It brings light to hidden or unconscious aspects and offers insight into any self-sabotaging patterns created from trauma-related experiences.

It's important to share that master plant medicine is not for everyone and should be respected and taken in a sacred space and facilitated by someone who understands it on all levels and has strong relationships with the plants, someone who can assist in safely integrating the experience before and after.

MY PERSONAL EXPERIENCE

The awareness and understanding that comes from master plant medicines is truly exciting. The shamans of the world have been working with these potent plants from the beginning of time and understand how essential they are to the healing of humanity, and I have had quite a few experiences with plant medicine myself. I went to Iquitos in Peru, which is in the middle of the Amazon and can only be reached by plane, and walked the streets looking for someone who could take me to an indigenous medicine person to facilitate an ayahuasca ceremony. I eventually connected with a guide who agreed to take me, along with an Australian man who wanted to come as well. We spent three days travelling down the Amazon on a boat and sleeping in hammocks with the locals, finally arriving at our destination and then spending another three hours travelling further into the jungle on a smaller canoe. We were welcomed into a small village then prepared to travel on foot deep into the Amazon jungle.

It was one of the most difficult and intense experiences of my life, a true vision quest. As the shaman wanted us to spend some time in the forest before we took any journeys with the ayahuasca medicine we walked through dense rainforest in our gumboots deep into the jungle, spending a few days there before heading back to the main camp. One evening the Australian man, our guide and me gathered in a small hut

to await the shaman's arrival. One by one people from the village turned up and I thought for a moment that we were perhaps going to be the night's entertainment; however, they were also there to experience the potent ancient sacrament.

Me after my ayahuasca ceremony in the Amazon jungle.

The shaman was an older man with a very gentle energy about him; he couldn't speak English so our guide acted as interpreter. We sat in circle while the shaman prepared the sacred space, singing ancient songs, burning palo santo and cleansing the energy in the room by shaking a branch from a local tree. It was a surreal experience on many levels and I was super excited to take this journey, but I was also feeling a little apprehensive and scared about what was to come. I was handed the plant medicine and asked to pray over the ayahuasca with my intentions and communicate with the spirit of the plant. I drank the medicine and sat quietly and patiently while it did its thing.

As the ayahuasca started to expend my consciousness I felt a deep connection with the trees and nature, at the same time realising how far away I had got from this natural relationship. I realised that being brought up in the city and the stressful life I was living had me surrounded in a shell of stressful energy that kept me separate from the inherent healing energy of nature. I felt totally disconnected from myself, and knew it was time to start doing things differently in my life.

As I went deep into my journey I felt quite ill and needed to purge the energy from my body, which I did. I was struggling quite a bit in my journey and the shaman could see this, so he came over to help me. What happened next blew me away on so many levels: he made a cross with his thumb on my temple and placed his mouth right up on the side of my face, and literally started sucking toxic energy out of my mind; I could feel it leave my brain. The shaman turned around and spat out a liquid on the ground. He then did this to the other side of my face and the crown of my head. He then spent time praying over me and cleansing me with ancient songs and the tree branches.

On my ayahuasca journey, which lasted for around seven hours, I went through a life review and could see very clearly what wasn't working – especially around many beliefs, thoughts and patterns I had created that were causing a huge disconnection with myself and creating depression, anxiety and a world of pain. It was such a channelling, life-expanding and healing journey on many levels but particularly mentally. After the first session I rested and slept for hours, after which we were asked to bathe in the river for cleansing.

I stayed in the Amazon for an extra week so I could work with this powerful medicine and the shamans to further my healing journey. It took many years for me to truly integrate my ayahuasca journey in the Amazon, but the plant medicine did immediately heal my mental state of being on a deep level. Before I had had my experience with ayahuasca my nervous system was on high alert and I suffered a lot of anxiety and mental torment and my short-term memory was really compromised. After the experience I felt as though it had healed my mind and nervous systems to a point where I was able to live from a deeper place within myself and my mind wasn't constantly racing and attacking me all the time.

I no longer live off nervous energy to get me through the day. At the time I didn't truly know the power of this medicine, but I now deeply understand how much this sacred plant has helped me. I still have a very sensitive mental state of being and it's a work in progress to keep it balanced and calm; however, I have more awareness and control over my thoughts and feel a calmer presence within myself.

Twenty years after my first ayahuasca session I started to tune back in to plant medicine and had an opportunity to microdose psilocybin, the active ingredient in magic mushrooms. There is an abundance of case studies and very positive information emerging about the use of this medicine to treat addiction, post-traumatic stress disorder, anxiety and depression. Modern-day medicine is starting to catch up with the ancient ways and honour and understand how powerful this medicine is and how it can help humanity, particularly as antidepressants and similar medicines are not working as effectively as first thought.

People are searching for other medicines to help and many are finding healing and relief in powerful sacred plants that have been honoured and understood by the shamanic medicine people of the world for thousands of years. Currently psilocybin is classed as a Schedule 1 drug, a drug with no accepted medical use and a high potential for abuse, but I believe that will change as the need for it and the understanding of the part it can play in healing increase. There are some wonderful people in the forefront of getting these medicines legalised for therapy use, and I believe these sacred plants and sacraments need to be respected and the intention and setting for taking them needs to be very clear, as this plays a very important role in how the medicine

is experienced. They should be used as sacred sacrament and medicine and not as party drugs, as they are powerful, life-changing medicines that require support and assistance to integrate the process before and after the experience.

Microdosing means taking a very small amount of the mushroom to receive its medicinal benefits without experiencing psychedelic effects. Magic mushrooms have been used by our ancestors for thousands of years; they grow in harmony with us and are found all around the world. My experiences with microdosing have been life changing and deeply healing on many levels, and my intention with taking them was to help me make better choices in my life when it came to being kind to myself and doing positive things that allowed me to nurture and care for myself instead of sabotaging and punishing myself with negative behaviours.

The medicine of the mushrooms helps to dissolve the walls around neuro pathways in the brain. For example, when you have a thought it creates a neuro pathway, and when you action that thought the pathway becomes stronger. When the thought is repeated the pathway becomes stronger and your mind defaults back to the same thought pattern, and the more you think it the stronger the pathway and the thicker the walls become. This pathway eventually becomes a strong thought pattern that creates an addiction to that thought or action, which can be very helpful when you're learning something new and mastering it – although it can act as the opposite and not be so helpful if it's a negative pattern.

Psilocybin allows the old neuro pathways to dissolve and fires fresh energy into the brain, offering new thought patterns that are more aligned to positive feelings. It also helps stimulate the creative part of the brain and offers an overall sense of inner well-being. My experiences have been subtle yet powerful and have helped me to make more positive choices in my life with regard to being kind to myself, a lifelong journey.

Plant medicine provides a way forward for humanity and is certainly an alternative to traditional antidepressants for managing depression and trauma-related issues as well as other imbalances in the mind, body and spirit. I don't, however, think it's for everyone, and feel you need to be deeply called by the plant before you take this sacred healing journey together. It is a potent sacrament for healing and spiritual awakening and needs to be honoured and respected.

CRYSTAL ALLY

GREEN TOURMALINE

Green tourmaline is a lovely green stone that assists you in creating a deep connection with Mother Earth, her medicines and nature spirits. It:

- ⫷ assists in shamanic journeying to meet the plant, flower and herb devas

- ⫷ opens you to receiving the healing energy and wisdom held deep within the earth

- ⫷ purifies and strengthens the nervous system

- ⫷ balances and harmonises the heart chakra, allowing for healing around any old wounds of the heart

- ⫷ creates forgiveness and understanding

- ⫷ sets you free from the restraints of fear

- ⫷ encourages honouring of yourself and others.

YOUR CEREMONY

This ceremony will enhance and create a connection with the spirit of a plant you would like to have a deeper relationship with:

- Once you have decided which plant, flower or herb you would like a deeper connection with, sit in a sacred place, hold the plant and close your eyes and start to relax your mind and focus on your breath. If you can't physically hold the plant then visualise yourself holding it.
- Call in the spirit of the plant.
- Take a few moments to breathe the energy of the plant into your heart and send the energy around your body.
- Start to connect with its spirit and breathe with its energy.
- Ask the plant spirit to share information about how this medicine can help you.
- Thank the spirit of the plant and give an offering of some sort: a song, prayer, mantra, piece of your hair or nails – anything you feel guided to offer as thanks and gratitude to the ally for its guidance and healing.

Record your experience.

_____

_____

_____

_____

_____

_____

_____

CHAPTER 7

MOTHER EARTH

Mother Earth is a conscious living, breathing being whom we are deeply connected with at all times; we are born into her womb, and when we pass our blood and bones return to her body. She was called Mother Earth by many who came before us and they truly understood her role as our earth mother: she holds the energy of unconditional love and the divine feminine. Her energy sustains, nurtures, warms and holds us and supports our existence on this plant.

THE MEDICINE OF MOTHER EARTH

The earth is our true mother as we walk our journey through life. Over the years, with the progress and expansion of the world, concrete has been laid over her, life has become fast paced and we are disconnected from the earth and the world around us. In truth our heart connection to the earth can never be severed, but for most of us and the lives we live we have created a disconnection in our mind and awareness. We spend many

hours on electronic devices and live in concrete jungles far from a natural connection with earth, and when we are disconnected from Mother Earth we are disconnected from ourselves.

As you strengthen and become more conscious of your relationship with the earth you become more connected to yourself. Mother Earth gifts you powerful healing energy and encourages you to delve deeply into the wisdom that lies within you. She is your mother, your nourishment physically, emotionally and mentally, and she constantly shares her love and compassion with you and invites you to sit deep in her womb while she holds and nurtures you. By reconnecting with the earth you will feel more at home and at peace within your being. She is calling you home to your heart and asks you to tread gently upon the land.

MY PERSONAL EXPERIENCE

Mr Turts, the turtle I rescued who shared his wisdom with me.

I have experienced many profound heart-opening connections with our beautiful mother Gaia throughout my shamanic journey, but one that stands out strongly in my heart is my first sweat lodge. A sweat lodge is an ancient traditional Native American healing ceremony. The lodge is shaped like a dome, with tree branches as the foundation and blankets laid over the top. Sacred stones are heated up for hours in a fire and placed in the centre of the lodge. Usually four rounds in the lodge are undertaken, each one honouring the direction, elements, grandmother and grandfather spirits and any other earth medicine you are working with. Hours are spent in the sweat lodge to purify and heal, the intention being that you are held in the womb of Mother Earth and are deeply connected with her heart.

Every sweat lodge I experienced gave me profound spiritual healing and a huge cleansing of my mind, body and spirit. The experience in my first sweat lodge was the time I felt most connected with Mother Earth: I sensed her love and presence within and around me and felt completely held and nurtured in this knowing, like the deepest unconditional love imaginable.

Late one afternoon 13 people including me gathered on the land of a lovely lady who lived in the Northern Rivers of New South Wales. This particular sweat lodge was a women-only naked sweat; however, not all sweats are taken with clothes off. Once we had entered into the sacred space inside the sweat lodge it was as though we were one soul, one being, one cell. The sweat lasted for four hours, during which time we cried, laughed, prayed, screamed, sang and released together. One woman sang then we all sang, then someone laughed and we all laughed. It was as though we were a collective consciousness that was helping and supporting each other's experience.

I sensed an energy building inside me and knew it was my turn to receive. After a little resistance the energy broke free and I started to weep, and the others wailed with me. Memories flashed in of being in my mother's womb and how challenging that had been for me, as my mum was a very sick woman at the time. I could feel her pain and struggling and realised I had taken them on as my own. I didn't blame my mother for the pain, as she had done the best she could with what she had at the time.

There was sweat pouring out of my body as I cried from every cell of my being, and the tears fell upon the earth. I felt as though I was lying

on my mother's breast; however, I was lying on the land and being held by Mother Gaia and I could feel her presence, heart and unconditional love. As my awareness of my mother's stress filled every cell of my being I was able to release this old stale energy through my tears. It was replaced with the pure love of Mother Earth. I felt completely held and nurtured and understood that our Earth Mother Gaia loved me unconditionally, and that when I connected with her energy it healed the wounds around my mother.

After the session in the sweat lodge we gathered in the house for tea, and all I wanted to do was go home and be in my own energy. I felt completely open and vulnerable like a newborn baby.

The day before the sweat while driving home from a drum birthing I rescued a turtle on the road that had been hit by a car. I felt blessed to have this beautiful turtle in my home that I was able to nurture back to health. After the sweat lodge and having the turtle show up at this time I started to realise that turtle medicine is all about connecting with Mother Earth and healing the wounds of the mother. It was no random occurrence that I had been given an opportunity to connect with the turtle medicine at this exact time; it came into my life to support me through the healing around my mother and was confirmation that deep tangible healing was at hand.

Around this same time I was gifted a piece of diopside, indicating this medicine was also about healing mother wounds and connecting deeply with the earth. There are no mistakes, and universe and earth energies are always supporting us and guiding us on our paths.

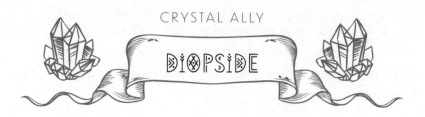

CRYSTAL ALLY

DIOPSIDE

Diopside is a pale greenish to greenish grey crystal that assists in connecting with the heart of Mother Earth. It also:

⫷ assists in receiving Mother Earth's healing
energy around any mother issues

⫷ allows an opening to receive and nurture yourself

⫷ holds you deep in love while you journey to the core of
your childhood issues for transformation and healing

⫷ brings awareness to deep-seated rejection issues
that stem from birth or early childhood

⫷ assists in releasing fear and feeling of abandonment

⫷ helps you identify trauma carried from the womb.

YOUR CEREMONY

There is an abundance of ceremonies you can facilitate to connect deeply with Mother Earth, and the one I offer here uses a medicine drum. If you don't have a medicine drum you can use two wooden sticks to carry out the process:

- Find a peaceful place somewhere on the land where you won't be disturbed.
- Close your eyes and play your drum or sticks along to the rhythm of your heartbeat.
- Connect deeply with your heartbeat then connect it with the heartbeat of the earth.
- Send love deep into the earth and thank her for everything she offers you: security, food, grounding and support.
- Feel deep gratitude for Mother Earth.
- Spend as long as you like in this space, drumming to your heartbeat and connecting with Mother Earth, making sure you open yourself to receive the love and healing she sends to you.
- Thank Mother Earth and give an offering of some sort: a song, prayer, mantra, piece of your hair or nails – anything you feel guided to offer as thanks and gratitude to the ally for its guidance and healing.

Record your experience.

_____

_____

_____

_____

CHAPTER 8

FATHER SKY

In ancient myths and teachings Father Sky was the first to be created from the universe, followed by Mother Earth, and together they created everything in between that exists on the earth.

THE MEDICINE OF FATHER SKY

Father Sky is our connection with spirit and the heavens, and to the higher realms. The medicine of the sky is also that of the masculine, and masculine energy is all about action, solution and protection and providing solutions.

When you connect with the spirit of Father Sky you will be open to heal the wounds of the father as well as those of your masculine energy. Males and females all have within them masculine and feminine energy, and the ultimate goal is to heal and balance them both.

MY PERSONAL EXPERIENCE

To be completely transparent with you I want to share the fact that my connection with this element is a work in progress. I have not had an experience with sky medicine, but I will outline what I understand about it.

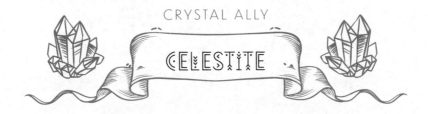

CRYSTAL ALLY

CELESTITE

Celestite is associated with divine power
and increases understanding. It also:

⤡ assists in connecting with the aspects of the masculine

⤡ helps to heal the wounds of the masculine

⤡ facilitates a deep connection to the divine source

⤡ encourages acceptance of the flow of
life and that all is in divine order

⤡ promotes deep soul healing and transformation

⤡ creates a space of peace, calm,
tranquillity and deep relaxation

⤡ assists with connection and communication
with the angelic realm.

YOUR CEREMONY

This ceremony is best performed outside under the sky. If you have a piece of celestite it would be a great idea to work with it in the ceremony but, if not, you can call in the deva and spirit of this energy. For this ceremony to connect with Father Sky:

- Sit or lie on a rug or mat and get comfortable.
- Close your eyes and set the intention to connect into the powerful spirit of Father Sky.
- Take a few moments to call in the deva of celestite, or if you have a physical crystal place it on your heart and take a few moments to connect with it.
- Call upon the spirit of Father Sky, and see yourself floating high up into the sky and sitting on a cloud.
- Bring your awareness to your breath, making sure you take long, deep breaths. As you inhale breathe in the energy of the sky, and as you exhale send this energy into every cell of your body.
- Breathe like this for a few minutes as you completely connect with and embody the medicine of Father Sky.
- Ask for a direct experience: Father Sky may come and talk to you, give you a message, share wisdom or give you a healing.
- Stay there until you feel the experience is complete.
- Thank the spirit of Father Sky and the deva of celestite and give an offering of some sort: a song, prayer, mantra, piece of your hair or nails – anything you feel guided to offer as thanks and gratitude to the ally for their guidance and healing.

Record your experience.

_____

_____

_____

_____

_____

_____

_____

_____

_____

_____

_____

_____

_____

_____

_____

_____

_____

_____

_____

_____

_____

_____

_____

_____

CHAPTER 9

GRANDMOTHER MOON

The powerful moon has an abundance of energy to offer to the world and her connection runs deep. She controls the tides and waterways on the planet and can also greatly affect your emotional state. She holds a deep wisdom and embodies the energy of the divine feminine and invites you to tap into and align with this energy within yourself, helping you to heal any wounds. She can illuminate the things held deep in your shadow self and offer awareness on how to bring them into the light and consciousness, offering healing to the hidden parts of your psyche. Grandmother Moon also helps you get in touch with your internal cycles and attune to the rhythm of your soul. Throughout the years, months, weeks, days and hours you spend in your life, you have your own internal cycles: at times you will be in your full moon phase and at other times in your dark moon phase and everything in between.

THE MEDICINE OF GRANDMOTHER MOON

The moon's various phases create different energies, and when you understand what part of the cycle you are in it will help you attune to your phase and not resist this natural internal flow. For example, when you feel full of energy and sociable and want to get out into the world and are inspired to create you may be in your full moon phase, and when you feel like you want to hide in your cave and rest you could be in your dark moon phase.

We tend to judge ourselves if we are not in the full moon phase all the time, but it's normal to have days when you don't have much energy although we tend to feel the need to push ourselves to make things happen. The mastery comes in understanding what phase you are in and honouring it, and Grandmother Moon medicine can definitely help you to do this.

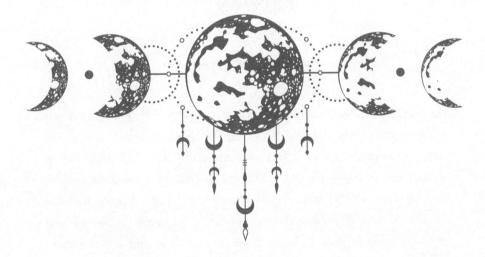

Full moons occur in different astrological signs each month, so when you are connecting with the moon you can also draw on this medicine and frequency. Here is a list of the energy that comes with a full moon for each sign:

- Aries: courage, dynamism, optimism
- Taurus: reliability, stability, groundedness
- Gemini: adaptability, curiosity, gentleness
- Cancer: empathy, strong imagination, tenacity
- Leo: creativity, drama, self-confidence
- Virgo: hard work, loyalty, kindness
- Libra: diplomacy, sociability, harmony
- Scorpio: braveness, resourcefulness, emotional intuitiveness
- Sagittarius: passion, assertiveness, freedom
- Capricorn: practicality, self-assurance, groundedness
- Aquarius: strength, individuality, independence
- Pisces: imagination, artistry, wisdom.

MY PERSONAL EXPERIENCE

Who doesn't love a full moon and go a little loopy around this time? One memorable moment I had with the Grandmother Moon was during a special super moon called a blood moon, which occur only around twice a year. I decided to burn some old journals and honour and connect with this significant energy. As I sat near the fire connecting with her I could feel a very strong presence, and it was as though she was speaking with me inside my head in thoughts rather than spoken words. The thoughts said: 'Rachelle, you don't have to be in your full moon all the time. When I am in my full moon I am in my glory and when I am in my dark moon I am in the presence and energy of my dark cycle. If I was to be in my full moon all the time the world would be in chaos.'

I sat with these thoughts for a while and processed what they meant for me. I realised I was a person who always wanted to feel happy, upbeat and vibrant, finding it difficult to experience more challenging emotions such as sadness and stillness. The moon shared with me that it was time to connect with the other phases and cycles within my being, to attune to my own flow and allow those parts of my psyche that contained more

challenging emotions to be present just as I did with the joyful ones. Grandmother Moon offered me support as I felt into the unseen parts of myself that I had denied. After my experience with moon energy I came to the understanding that connecting with your internal cycles was a big part of her medicine, and when I could connect with this energy within myself deep healing was experienced.

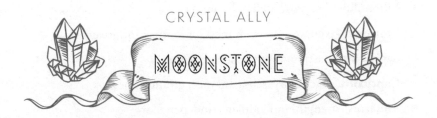

CRYSTAL ALLY

MOONSTONE

Moonstone, which is found worldwide and is valued for its blue to white moonlight sheen, harvests the energy of the moon. It also:

⟨⟨ connects you deeply to your feminine energy and heals any imbalances in this area

⟨⟨ enhances fertility and the planting of new seeds, ideas and inspirations

⟨⟨ creates fresh beginnings, directions and creativity

⟨⟨ connects you with the energy of the moon and her cycles and the ebb and flow of life, bringing you into balance

⟨⟨ encourages you to open yourself to intimacy

⟨⟨ assists in birthing new projects and creations.

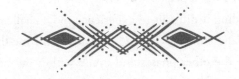

YOUR CEREMONY

This ceremony for connecting with the moon can be carried out during any phase:

- Prepare a small fire on the earth, making sure it's contained in a safe area.
- Set the intention that you are creating it as an offering to Grandmother Moon.
- Light the fire and send your good intentions and love to Grandmother Moon.
- Sit by your sacred fire and ask for a message from Grandmother Moon, and be open to receiving her wisdom and energy.
- Play a drum, rattle or stick or simply sit in silence and be bathed by the medicine of the moon.
- Offer thanks and give an offering of some sort: a song, prayer, mantra, piece of your hair or nails – anything you feel guided to offer as thanks and gratitude to the ally for its guidance and healing.

Record your experience.

_____

_____

_____

_____

_____

_____

_____

CHAPTER 10

GRANDFATHER SUN

Grandfather Sun is the masculine energy to Grandmother Moon. The sun offers light, warmth and energy to Mother Earth and illuminates the path as you walk your earthly journey. The energy and light of the sun starts and ends the day and we would not be able to survive without it, as the energy of the sun brings life to everything on the physical plane.

THE MEDICINE OF GRANDFATHER SUN

Whenever you need more energy and life force in your life call upon Grandfather Sun to light up your world. The spiritual awareness of the sun is the connection to source energy, divine light, the great central sun and the god source. When you connect with the sun you connect into Christ light and consciousness.

MY PERSONAL EXPERIENCE

My experiences with Grandfather Sun have allowed for a deeper connection with the god source as it's been deeply personal and soul moving. When I attended my first crystal workshop I was introduced to universal source energy as the great central sun, and it was the first time I had felt a deep connection with this universal energy for a long time.

I had been brought up as a Catholic and had a strong aversion to the word 'God' due to the way in which I was taught to view this universal source energy, so being introduced to the essence of the Great Central Sun in this new way that I felt deeply connected to had a profound effect on me. It helped me move beyond my resistance and perception to a place where I realised that no matter what we call god source energy it comes from the same place and has the same fundamental essence. This awareness allowed me to expand myself to embrace my own deep connection to God. Our connection to our god or Grandfather Sun is deeply personal, and we each have a unique experience with it.

CRYSTAL ALLY

GOLDEN CALCITE

Calcite is one of the most abundant minerals on earth. Golden calcite will give you mental clarity and also:

◆ invoke the energy of the sun

◆ open your crown chakra and draw in the light and love of the universe

◆ promote deep relaxation and calm your mind

◆ illuminate your soul

◆ connect you deeply and fully with the wisdom of the cosmos.

YOUR CEREMONY

This ceremony will bring more light and energy to your life. It would be a good idea to work with some golden calcite if you have some, but if not you can call in its energy:

- Fill up a glass with water.
- Find a comfortable place inside or outside where you will not be disturbed.
- Close your eyes and take a few moments to connect with your crystal, breathing this energy into your heart.
- Call upon the energy of the sun with the intention of connecting deeply.
- Visualise the sun filling up your glass of water with energy for around 5 minutes.
- Drink the water and feel the energy of the sun filling up every cell of your body.
- Send the sun energy into anywhere in your body that requires energy or healing.
- Send the energy of Grandfather Sun into anything in your life that requires energy or rejuvenation and see this sun energy permeate its rays of light into your chosen creation.
- See it transform in your mind's eye.
- Stay there for a few minutes until you feel the energy totally infusing and bathing your visualisation.
- Take a moment to thank Grandfather Sun and give an offering of some sort: a song, prayer, mantra, piece of your hair or nails – anything you feel guided to offer as thanks and gratitude to the ally for its guidance and healing.

Record your experience.

_____

_____

_____

_____

_____

_____

_____

_____

_____

_____

_____

_____

_____

_____

_____

_____

_____

_____

_____

_____

_____

_____

CHAPTER 11

THE ELEMENTS

The power and medicine of the elements has been understood for thousands of years and is the foundation of ancient Hindu Ayurvedic and Chinese acupuncture practices, along with being the basis of pagan and Celtic traditions. The shamans of the world understood the elements and worked closely with these aspects to attain a place of balance within the mind, body and spirit.

THE MEDICINE OF THE ELEMENTS

All living things that exist on the physical plane, including us and Mother Earth, are made up of and connected with the five building blocks of creation called the elements: fire, air, water, earth and spirit. Each element has unique energy and qualities that can affect us physically, emotionally, mentally and spiritually. The elements have a consciousness and are alive in each and every one of us, and by understanding, invoking, connecting and integrating these powerful elements we can strengthen our relationship and utilise this connection to create healing and wholeness.

Our inter-connectedness to the five elements allows our connection with the sacredness of existence. Over the years as we have become disconnected from nature we have become separated from this powerful source, which has created an imbalance and disharmony. In our physical reality we are in constant connection and communication with the elements, inviting and reminding us to maintain a state of harmony. Creating this connection is as simple as invoking, integrating and understanding deeply what each element has to offer.

The wisdom of the elements lives within us and is available at any moment, as they make up the manifestation of our physical body: earth is our body, water is our blood, air is our breath and fire is our spirit. The goal is to master these elements and obtain and create a state of balance with them, for when balance is achieved an alignment takes place and we connect to the vibrant energy and vitality that is offered.

When the elements in nature are balanced a storm is created that allows for cleansing and renewal. The same process happens within our physical bodies: when the elements are in balance an internal storm is created and cleansing and healing occurs as the physical body aligns and heals itself.

When an element is out of balance it can manifest in different ways. To get a clear idea of how this works, I have provided a list of the traits that occur when the element is out of balance; the minus sign (–) identifies characteristics that occur when the element is lacking, while the plus sign (+) identifies characteristics that occur when there is too much of the element. Later in the book I will share how to work with crystals to balance the elements in the body.

The element of fire

Fire is the element of spirit and great creativity and initiates action, transformation and change.

> **Qualities of the fire element:** creativity, warmth, protection, sun, action, warrior, dynamism, expansion, masculinity, purification, healing, expression, will, success, transformation, sex, passion, movement, activity, dancing, strength, courage.

Below are the effects associated with the fire element.

> **Balanced:** courage, creativity, passion, strength, power, intuition, empowerment, manifestation.
>
> **Imbalanced:**
>
> | | |
> |---|---|
> | – Lack of energy | + Anxiety |
> | – Sexual addiction | + Self-abuse |
> | – Addictions | + Jealousy |
> | – Poor digestion | + Destructive, aggressive |
> | – Lack of creative flair | + Brash |
> | – Lack of courage | + Rude, abrupt |
> | – Disempowerment | + Overly controlling |
> | – Lack of intuition | + Outspoken, loud |
> | – Inability to manifest | + Attention seeking |

Water balances the intensity of fire and air enhances it.

The element of air

The air element, which connects you with your mental processes, has freedom of movement, expansion and activity, creating new ideas and visualisation.

> **Qualities of the air element:** mental stimulation, inspiration, new ideas, vision, communication, singing, clarity, teaching, thinking, imagination, wisdom, fresh beginnings, organisation, travel, messages, connection to spirit.

Below are the effects associated with the air element.

> **Balanced:** spiritual awareness, new projects and ideas, flexibility, creativity, clear communication, joy, freedom, feeling vibrant and alive, leadership.
>
> **Imbalanced:**
> - Suppressed emotion
> - Lack of vision
> - Lack of mental stimulation
> - Lack of imagination
> - Disconnection with spirit and guidance
> - Inability to communicate
> - Lack of joy
> - Lack of direction
>
> + Frustration, anxiety
> + Aggression, anger
> + Scattered mind
> + Critical
> + Spiritually mad
> + Outspoken
> + Overexcitable
> + Controlling, changeable

Earth balances the intensity of air and air enhances it.

The element of water

The water element connects you with your emotions
and intuition and invites you to connect with your flow.

> **Qualities of the water element:** feelings, love, flowing movement,
> reflection, cleansing, compassion, connection, surrender,
> receiving, forgiveness, purification, letting go, healing, friendship,
> partnership, mystery, dreaming.

Below are the effects associated with the water element.

> **Balanced:** open heart, compassion, devotion, forgiveness,
> tranquillity, peacefulness, contentment, emotional balance, healthy
> boundaries, openness.
>
> **Imbalanced:**
>
> | | |
> |---|---|
> | – Laziness | + Sensitivity |
> | – Instability | + Run from conflict |
> | – Frigidity | + Unhealthy boundaries |
> | – Inability to express emotions | + Reaction |
> | – Analysing feelings | + Depression |
> | – Relationship withdrawal | + Co-dependence |
> | – Closed heart, cold, no empathy | + Overcaring |
> | – Hard to forgive, holding grudges | + Overemotional |
> | – Lack feelings or emotions | + Lack of personal boundaries |

Fire balances the intensity of water and water enhances it.

The element of earth

The earth element is the most physical and grounding
of the elements and relates mostly to the material world
and physical body. It has the power to ground and manifest
things into the physical plane and is our connection to the earth and the
healing, loving energy of the mother.

Qualities of the earth element: Mother Earth, womb, feminine,
goddess, nurturing, healing, wisdom, knowledge, birth, death,
transformation, nature, home, family, receiving, vulnerability,
grounding, stability, nourishment, food, prosperity, abundance.

Below are the effects associated with the earth element.

Balanced: openness, compassion, physical health, concentration,
high energy, groundedness, self-assurance.

Imbalanced:

– Laziness	+ Self-sabotage
– Inability to make decisions	+ Stubbornness
– Inability to stay focused	+ Control
– Eating disorders	+ Inflexibility
– Obsessiveness	+ Rigidity

Air balances the intensity of earth and earth enhances it.

The element of spirit

The element of spirit is our connection to source, 'I am' presence, universe energy, the cosmos and the creator. It is our connection to all that is.

> **Qualities of the spirit element:** god/goddess, spirit, cosmos, universal love, wisdom, oneness, divine connection, unity, healing, awakening, transformation.

Below are the effects associated with the spirit element.

> **Balanced:** divine union with source, clarity, pure channel, wisdom, bliss, wholeness, lightness of being, spiritual awareness, clear direction, inner peace, god/goddess energy.
>
> **Imbalanced:** confusion, ungrounded, disconnected from reality, disconnected from self and source, lack of spirit, lack of love, joy and peace, lack of direction.

MY PERSONAL EXPERIENCE

It was while I was in Peru with Edwin that I was introduced to the power of the elements, but it wasn't until after that sacred journey that my understanding of and connection with the elements became deeper and stronger and I was able to fully embody the medicine.

As my interest grew stronger the element spirits started to connect with me and show me what they were all about. They are very much alive and are here to guide and share their energy and medicine with us on our journeys. My favourite element would have to be water, and one of my biggest loves is spending time at the beach. Walking on the beach has always been medicine for my soul as it fills every cell of my being with joy.

One glorious summer's day I went with my friend and beautiful dog Gaia to a dog beach for a walk. We cruised up the beach, enjoying the magical day, when suddenly the wind started to blow. Wind is my least favourite element, as it can at times stir up and amplify my not so comfortable emotions. According to my birth chart I am made up of a lot of air, so an extra wind element can tend to push me out of balance.

During our walk I had been in the most wonderful peaceful mood, but as the wind blew I started to feel angry and frustrated and my friend sensed that something was happening. She walked further up the beach and left me in my own space. I could feel something huge stirring inside of me, like a spiritual experience was about to happen as everything started to become brighter and more amplified. I was invited to connect with the wind instead of fighting it, to allow it to wash through me and surrender to it. I then heard a voice telling me to breathe, so I knelt down with my hands and knees on the sand and started to focus on my breathing. I took some long, deep breaths and became one with my breathing and also one with the wind.

I usually resisted the wind, but this time I dropped in and flowed with the process instead of getting frustrated, allowing it to wash over and move through me as I became one with the element. I could feel the power and strength of the sacred wind spirit within me when suddenly the water from the ocean came up and splashed over my hands. I wondered how that had happened as I was far back from the waves; nevertheless, the water had made its way to me. I became more aware of what was happening

around me and realised that a storm was brewing: there was lightning out at sea and it had started to rain, and I found myself in the middle of a pretty powerful storm. The incredible thing was that the storm had just formed over the top of me and I was in the centre of it.

I felt a strong sense to take off all my clothes and get into the ocean, so I did just that. As I stood with my arms out and surrendered to the experience I felt deeply at one with the water, the wind, the lightning and the sand. I had embodied all the elements in balance inside of me, which had created a storm and balance in the elements outside of me. I felt a huge sense of peace and power at the same time, and I cried and cried and released a whole lot of old stale energy that had been held in my body and mind. It was a powerful and profound experience that lasted about 10 minutes before everything started to settle and the storm drifted away.

I was still standing, naked, in the water. I could hear a voice coming from beyond the sand dunes but luckily it was my friend and dog. We walked back to the car in silence, both knowing instinctively that what had happened was very special and sacred. It took some time for me to come back into my body and integrate the process, and as I drove home I continued to cry and release and allowed the energy to nurture and heal me.

I didn't truly understand this experience at the time but I came to realise on a deep level that the elements are alive within us and we can work with them to create healing and balance in our lives.

Crystal allies

Crystals can play a big role in the integration of and connection with the elements and act as allies. Every crystal has all of the elements within them, although usually one element is dominant. Crystals can assist you to align to the medicine and consciousness of the elements. The following pages contain lists of the crystals that align with each element along with an explanation of my understanding of each element, which will hopefully guide you to having your own experience with each element so you can create your own connection to this medicine and discover what it means to you.

Calling upon and being energetically bathed in each of the elements and consciously working with them will assist you deeply in your connection and understanding. As you get a deeper understanding and awareness of

the elements you can work with the crystals to create balance. The key is to balance the element with the crystals; for example, if you have too much fire energy you should stay away from crystals that hold lots of fire and work with water crystals, as water balances fire.

Fire element: sunstone

- connects with the energy of the divine source of all things, invoking great personal power in your life
- awakens self-empowerment, creating strength and courage
- activates rebirth
- facilitates transformation
- releases blockages and resistance to change
- rekindles your passion for life.

The crystals associated with the fire element assist in creation and manifestation, as they bring movement and action in the physical plane. They are: bixbite, black obsidian, calcite, carnelian, cinnabar, citrine, fire agate, heliodor, malachite, meteorite, nuummite, obsidian, rhodochrosite, rhodonite, sunstone, tiger's eye, topaz.

Balancing: if you want to bring in more of the fire element you would connect with fire crystals, and if you had too much fire you would connect with earth or water crystals to create a balance.

Air element: labradorite

- allows you to connect with the mystery and magic of life
- assists in awakening the magic of your soul
- brings deep awareness of your spiritual knowledge, allowing it to manifest in your day-to-day life
- provides spiritual insight
- supports you to integrate spiritual experiences into the physical world.

The crystals associated with the air element assist in stimulation of the mind and brain function, and support you in bringing through messages from the higher realms. They are: amethyst, angelite, azurite, cacoxenite, calcite, celestite, charoite, danburite, dumortierite, fluorite, iolite, kunzite, kyanite, labradorite, lapis lazuli, moonstone, scolecite, selenite, sodalite, sugilite, tourmaline.

Balancing: if you want to bring in more of the air element you would connect with air crystals, and if you had too much air you would connect with earth crystals to create a balance.

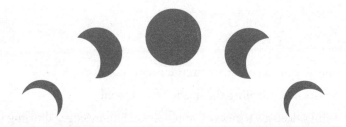

Water element: aquamarine

- facilitates clear communication and supports self-expression
- helps you connect with your emotions and speak truth from your heart
- assists in connecting with and expressing your wisdom and knowledge
- allows you to find your voice.

The crystals associated with the water element assist you in communicating your feelings and truth to others, allowing you to embody more love and compassion and help you to set healthy boundaries. They are: agate, amazonite, chalcedony, chrysocolla, chrysoprase, dioptase, emerald, Gaia stone, green tourmaline, hiddenite, kunzite, larimar, morganite, pink tourmaline, rhodochrosite, rose quartz.

Balancing: if you want to bring in more of the water element you would connect with water crystals, and if you had too much water you would connect with fire crystals to create a balance.

Earth element: mookaite jasper

- is often used in ceremonies and rituals
- encourages deep connection with the wisdom and ancestors of Australia
- assists in your journey into the spirit world and the Dreamtime
- helps you receive deep healing from the earth
- connects you with the heart of the earth.

The crystals associated with the earth element assist you to connect with the physical experience and to exist in the present moment, and keep you connected with and grounded on the earth. They are: amber, Apache tears, awakening crystal (elestial quartz), bixbite, black tourmaline, bloodstone, Boji/shaman stones, cuprite, diopside, galena, garnet, hematite, jade, jasper, jet, nuummite, obsidian, ocean jasper, onyx, peridot, petrified wood, pyrite, ruby.

Balancing: if you want to bring in more of the earth element you would connect with earth crystals, and if you had too much earth you would connect with air crystals to create a balance.

Spirit element: selenite

- is a powerful crystal that works as a vacuum cleaner to purify and cleanse your aura
- opens and stimulates your crown chakra and brings in the divine light of the cosmos, balancing the chakras
- encourages you to take powerful action in your life
- allows you to move forward in strength
- connects with your higher self and 'I am' presence
- shields your aura from any unwanted influences
- detoxifies your energy field.

The crystals that align with the spirit element are: amazonite, amethyst, ametrine, angelite, apophyllite, brazilianite, cacoxenite, celesite, charoite, cinnabar, danburite, fulgurite, golden calcite, labradorite, Libyan gold tektite, moldavite, natrolite, phenacite, pietersite, scolecite, Tibetan quartz, topaz.

YOUR
CEREMONIES

FÎRE ELEMENT CEREMONY

To connect with the element of fire, work with a piece of sunstone as an ally:

⋘ Safely create a fire or use a candle.

⋘ Close your eyes and connect with your crystal, asking it to act as an ally to help you connect with the spirit of fire.

⋘ Breathe the crystal's energy into your heart and send it around your body as you align with this vibration.

⋘ Light the fire or candle and call upon the spirits of fire, asking them to give you an experience of their energy.

⋘ Connect with the fire element within yourself and ask whether or not it is in balance. If it is not, ask what you need to do: think about what the fire element means to you and what your relationship is with fire.

⋘ Ask for a message from the fire spirit, then sit and be aware of what comes to you and be open to receiving it.

⋘ Stay there for as long as it feels comfortable to do so.

⋘ Thank the crystal and fire spirit for this experience and give an offering of some sort: a song, prayer, mantra, piece of your hair or nails – anything you feel guided to offer as thanks and gratitude to the ally for its guidance and healing.

Record your experience.

_____

_____

_____

_____

AIR ELEMENT CEREMONY

To connect with the element of air, work with a piece of labradorite as an ally. This exercise is best done outside in nature:

- Close your eyes and connect into your crystal, asking it to act as an ally to help you connect with the spirit of air.
- Breathe the crystal's energy into your heart and send it around your body as you align with this vibration.
- Call upon the spirits of air and ask them to give you an experience.
- Connect with the air element within yourself, your sacred breath, and ask whether or not the air element within you is in balance. If it is not, ask what you need to do: think about what the air element means to you and what your relationship is with air.
- Ask for a message from the air spirit, then sit and be aware of what comes to you and be open to receiving it.
- Stay there for as long as it feels comfortable to do so.
- Thank the crystal and air spirit for this experience and give an offering of some sort: a song, prayer, mantra, piece of your hair or nails — anything you feel guided to offer as thanks and gratitude to the ally for its guidance and healing.

Record your experience.

_____

_____

_____

_____

WATER ELEMENT CEREMONY

To connect with the water element, work with a piece of aquamarine as an ally. This exercise can be undertaken in or around the water:

- Close your eyes and connect into your crystal, asking it to act as an ally to help you connect with the spirit of water.
- Breathe the crystal's energy into your heart and send it around your body as you align with this vibration.
- Call upon the spirits of water and ask them to give you an experience.
- Connect with the water element within yourself and ask whether or not the water element within you is in balance. If it is not, ask what you need to do: think about what the water element means to you and what your relationship is with water.
- Ask for a message from the water spirit, then sit and be aware of what comes to you and be open to receiving it.
- Stay there for as long as it feels comfortable to do so.
- Thank the crystal and water spirit for this experience and give an offering of some sort: a song, prayer, mantra, piece of your hair or nails – anything you feel guided to offer as thanks and gratitude to the ally for its guidance and healing.

Record your experience.

_____

_____

_____

_____

_____
_____
_____
_____
_____
_____
_____
_____
_____
_____
_____
_____
_____
_____
_____
_____
_____
_____
_____
_____
_____
_____
_____
_____

EARTH ELEMENT CEREMONY

To connect with the earth element, work with a piece of mookaite jasper as an ally. This exercise is done best outside on the earth:

- Close your eyes and connect into your crystal, asking it to act as an ally to help you connect with Mother Earth.
- Breathe the crystal's energy into your heart and send it around your body as you align with this vibration.
- Call upon Mother Earth, asking her to give you an experience.
- Become aware of Mother Earth's heartbeat and of your own heartbeat. Spend a few minutes connecting your heart with the heart of Mother Earth.
- Ask whether or not the earth element within you is in balance. If not, ask what you need to do: think about what the earth element means to you and what your relationship is with earth.
- Ask for a message from Mother Earth, then sit and be aware of what comes to you and be open to receiving it.
- Stay there for as long as it feels comfortable to do so.
- Thank the crystal and Mother Earth for this experience and give an offering of some sort: a song, prayer, mantra, piece of your hair or nails – anything you feel guided to offer as thanks and gratitude to the ally for its guidance and healing.

Record your experience.

_____

_____

_____

SPIRIT ELEMENT CEREMONY

To connect with the spirit element, work with a piece of selenite as an ally. Then:

- Close your eyes and connect into your crystal, asking it to act as an ally to help you connect with the spirit element.
- Breathe the crystal's energy into your heart and send it around your body as you align with this vibration.
- Call upon the element of spirit and ask to be given an experience.
- Draw the golden light of spirit down from the heavens and into the crown of your head, then into every cell of your body. Spend a few minutes connecting.
- Ask whether or not the spirit element within you is in balance. If not, ask what you need to do: think about what the spirit element means to you and what your relationship is with spirit.
- Ask for a message from spirit, then sit and be aware of what comes to you and be open to receiving it.
- Stay there for as long as it feels comfortable to do so.
- Thank the crystal and spirit for this experience and give an offering of some sort: a song, prayer, mantra, piece of your hair or nails – anything you feel guided to offer as thanks and gratitude to the ally for its guidance and healing.

Record your experience.

_____

_____

_____

CHAPTER 12

MEDICINE TOOLS OF THE EARTH

Alongside working with the spirit and energy of earth medicine, animals and allies, medicine men and women also used the whole body of an animal and utilised the various parts in ceremonies, healing and rituals. They understood that everything is sacred, and when they connected with the physical part of the animal while honouring its spirit they could channel its medicine and energy for healing. It is a deeply sacred and spiritual act to work with animal medicine in this way and, although it's definitely not for everyone, if you are called to do so it will be a strong call from the animal's spirit and you will be guided in the process.

MEDICINE DRUMS

Medicine drums have been utilised by many cultures for a range of different purposes. In ceremonies the drumbeat was the heartbeat of the

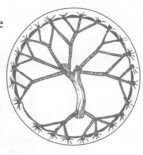

ceremony, and the energy of the drum lifted the vibration of its surroundings and allowed for the veils of the worlds to become thin so different dimensions could be accessed. When the drum is played you weave into a tapestry of healing energy that has been created over thousands of years from those who played before you.

Medicine drums were also used as tools in rites of passage and to celebrate and honour the community, ancestors and spirit world. A sacred Native American ceremony known as the 'sun dance' can last for weeks, and drums are the heart of the ritual and are played for the entire time. When the drums stop the ceremony is over.

Medicine drums are made from animal skins, each of which has a unique vibration and medicine, and when the drum is played the spirit and soul of that animal is called forth to share its energy. The most commonly used skins include those of deer, goats and kangaroos. Deer medicine offers the energy of gentleness, kindness and healing the heart; goat medicine offers the energy of confidence, being grounded and reaching to the highest of heights; and kangaroo medicine is all about letting go, moving forward and never looking back.

Drums create different energy depending on the intention and beat of the drum. There are many traditional songs and rhythms that invoke a range of different outcomes and energy depending on intention when played. Traditionally, drums have been used for thousands of years to support and assist people to enter a trance state. As the drum beats at a certain speed the left and the right hemispheres of the brain move into balance and the brain waves enter a theta state, which is a trance-like state in which we can connect with the spirit world to receive visions, guidance, wisdom and healing. A two-beat drum beat, which is referred to as the heart beat, is played with the intention of connecting with the heart of the earth, a sacred space in which healing and balance are obtained.

We are deeply connected with Mother Earth; however, over time we have poured concrete on the land and created a fast-paced world in which there seems to be a disconnection. This can happen in our minds but *never* in our hearts, and playing the heartbeat of the drum strengthens the

_____

Amber

_____

*Ancient healing
crystal*

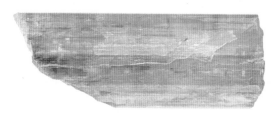

_____

Aquamarine

Black calcite

Black moonstone

Black obsidian

Black tourmaline

Boji/shaman stones

Celestite

Chrysotile

Cuprite

Diopside

Elestial quartz

Galena

Golden calcite

*Green
tourmaline*

Jet

Labradorite

Mookaite jasper

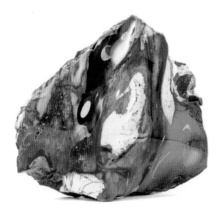

Moonstone

Nuummite

Petrified wood

Red jasper

Selenite

Shungite

Sunstone

connection with Mother Earth and opens you to receive the healing and unconditional love she has to offer. A heartbeat is the first thing you hear when you are in your mother's womb and you spend nine months being nurtured and kept alive by this rhythm. When this heartbeat is played on the drum you naturally attune with the heart of Mother Earth, which then opens you to a world of deep love and nurturing.

Drums have a large part to play in the journey process into the three worlds of shamanism. Trees are vortexes and entry points into these worlds, so it's no surprise that drums are usually made of wood. The animal skin is stretched over the wood to create the drum and the foundation of the drum becomes the connection to the trees, which is the entry point into the worlds. This is a union that goes hand in hand with the intention of dropping into the spirit of the sacred tree and the shamanic worlds.

FEATHERS

Feathers are one of the sacred medicine tools of shamans and healers. They have been working with the powerful medicine of feathers for thousands of years and understand how to utilise the gifts of feathers. Each bird has its own spirit and medicine to share, and when shamans work with sacred feathers they honour the bird and call in its spirit, embodying the energy of the bird and transferring this medicine through the feather. Feathers are also used as tools for cleansing the energy field as they invoke and call upon the element of air. Feathers are a symbol of protection and hope from the angelic realms; when you see a feather it can be a sign from a deceased loved one.

RATTLES

Rattles are another shamanic tool that the healers and shamans of the world would often create and work with for healing. They were made from animal body parts along with crystals, rocks, feathers and any other natural material the healer was drawn to. When you connect and work with sacred rattles you are invoking and calling upon all the different energies of the medicines that make up the tool. For example,

if you have a rattle with eagle feathers, bear fur and a nuummite crystal, when you connect with this rattle you will call upon the allies and energies of these medicines and work with them to invoke healing. Rattles can be used similarly to drums to take people into trance journeys, and they can also be used as a tool to honour and call upon beings from the spirit world.

STAFFS AND WANDS

A staff or wand is another healing tool of shamans and healers and is created by using materials from nature such as crystals, feathers, wood, seeds and animal parts. To make a staff or wand a shaman would be guided by the allies as to what medicine was to be placed on the tool, and a piece of wood is carved and crafted in sacred ceremony. This medicine is then collected as physical parts and hung from or connected with the wood holding this medicine within the staff or wand.

Staffs and wands are utilised for several different purposes: opening and holding sacred space to healing, protection, clearing, casting magic, connection to spirit and summoning spirit animals and medicines. Staffs were used in sacred ceremony and in personal meditation to activate and amplify the specific medicine of a person. The staff is a symbol of your journey and growth on a spiritual path and holds your power within it, grounding it into the physical plane.

Each initiation and awakening of your life's journey is reflected and represented on the staff, symbolised by a feather, crystal, carving or any other piece of nature that represents the wisdom and medicine that has been invoked. The staff is an outer manifestation of your power and can strongly assist in holding this power within you.

MY PERSONAL EXPERIENCE

My first-ever drumming circle sparked a deep passion and connection with drums. I love the energy drums create and the heart opening that's invoked when I play. For many years I worked with drums other people had made and I never thought I would ever make my own.

Around 10 years after beginning the Academy of Crystal Awakening I was guided to create a training opportunity in which I would offer my crystal and shamanic teachings to others so they could then teach. I had a vision of making each teacher their own medicine drum, as the drum had been such a powerful tool for me. As I dropped into this realisation I wondered for a moment who I was to make medicine drums, as they were not from my heritage and I had not studied their tradition. I later realised that medicine drums are used in many different cultures.

At the time it was important to honour the Native American lineage, so I found a lovely lady who facilitated drum making and I birthed my first drum to see how I felt and what showed up for me during the experience. I loved creating that drum, was deeply connected with the whole process and sensed that I had done it before.

After I birthed my first drum I was invited to take a 40-day journey with the medicine for which I would play my drum every day to assist with integrating and grounding in the energy. Some days I had powerful and profound awareness about the medicine and other days I didn't get much at all. Throughout the journey I had past-life realisations that I was a young, blind, Native American boy whose craft was making drums, and the drum journey birthed this past-life wisdom and knowledge of drum medicine and made it available to me in my present life. After this insight I felt it was okay to birth drums for others, and I also believed that when you do things from the heart with the intention for good you are empowered to create whatever medicine inspires and calls you. I love how on this healing path your soul and spirit of different medicine offers confirmations when connecting with them.

I was running a workshop a few weeks after birthing my first drum when a new guide came through for me whose name was Blue Elk. Three students at the workshop mentioned the words 'blue' and 'elk' on three different occasions, which I took to be strong confirmation. I later googled 'blue elk' and discovered an old Native American tale about a young blind, mute boy so I knew the information and wisdom I was receiving around the drum medicine was true, and it was a comforting confirmation that I was on the right track. I'm not a drum master, but a few years after this experience I was guided to facilitate drum-birthing workshops for people to create their own drums and awaken their personal wisdom and medicine.

PART III

CRYSTAL SHAMANISM PRACTITIONER HEALING

CHAPTER 13

SETTING A SACRED HEALING SPACE

Before you participate in any healings make sure the steps below are understood and followed. You will be working with subtle energy so it's vital to create a safe and clear sacred space for all types of healing. These steps will guide you in setting up a powerful healing space as you learn to open yourself to being a powerful channel and invoke your guides, angels and spirit helpers. When you facilitate healing you are never alone; you will have your spirit team ready and willing to assist, and these steps are a great way of invoking this guidance and support.

Even if you are doing the healing for yourself it's best to follow the steps below as you create your sacred healing space. Later in the book you will be offered several advanced healing processes and given the 13 steps of advanced healing for practitioners, which expands on the information given here and needs to be read before facilitating more advanced practices (see Chapter 27).

☄ Always work with crystals that have been cleansed and charged, and make sure you are both well hydrated.

☄ If you are doing a healing ceremony for someone else, connect with your client and discuss what they would like healing for.

☄ Prepare the healing space and clear any unwanted energies in the room by burning sage or setting an intention.

☄ Take a few moments to connect with your crystals and yourself.

☄ Call upon your healing guides, angels, animal allies and crystal devas. Set the healing space by saying an invocation that allows you to open to divine healing energy for the universe; there is one below, although you can use your own invocation. When you step into a sacred healing space you become a channel for healing energy, which is why it's important to call upon other helpers in the spirit world to guide the way.

☄ Set the intention that this healing is for the highest good of all.

☄ Quietly guide your client to close their eyes and focus on their breathing as they move deeply into relaxation, which will allow them to be open to receiving the energy.

☄ Visualise golden light streaming down from the universe through your crown chakra and into your heart, then offer and direct this energy to the earth. Expand the energy of love within your heart. Extend the loving energy down your arms and into your hands, which will open your heart so you can share the energy in the healing.

☄ Offer the chosen healing process; for example, crystal healing or soul, animal or crystal retrieval.

☄ To finish the healing, gently guide your client back into the room by saying something such as:

I call all aspects of the self back into the room, into the physical.

When you're ready, slowly open your eyes.

❧ Ask your client to share their experience and take time to listen to and support them with an open heart in unconditional love. Also, share with your client any messages you received in the healing from the universe, spirit or crystal devas.

Healing invocation

I invoke the love of the divine universe within my heart
I am a clear and pure channel
Love is my guide.

I invoke the love of the divine universe within my heart
I am a clear and pure channel
Love is my guide.

I invoke the love of the divine universe within my heart
I am a clear and pure channel
Love is my guide.

And I follow that love.

CHAPTER 14

HEALING CODE OF CONDUCT

Whether a practitioner is at the beginning of their healing journey or further along the pathway, it is important to always examine or revisit a code of conduct or code of ethics that ensures that as a group of healing professionals we are offering services that are of the highest good for all, and which come from a place of divine love and integrity. We all have unique gifts and personal styles that contribute to who we are and how we provide healings for others.

Clients accessing a healing service need to have a clear understanding of the process they are going to undertake and what may be involved for them so they can give informed consent. It is always advised that we only use techniques we have knowledge about and preferably have had support and training in using and/or may have experienced ourselves. Maintaining professional integrity will always support healing work; this includes honesty, sensitivity, genuineness, empathy for the experiences of

our clients, ongoing self-reflection and professional development. It also involves respecting the right to privacy and confidentiality of those who come to see us, who often share their vulnerability in the most trusting way. Our aim is not to stir up issues but rather to work with the emotional issues our clients initiate. We do not need to intrude unnecessarily on their privacy when seeking information.

In our dedication to our path as healers it is of crucial importance to maintain an ongoing commitment to professional development and future learning, including ongoing consultation with our healer colleagues and teachers. A commitment to continual learning will assure the quality of our service to our clients and create a clear awareness about our individual strengths and areas for potential growth. We have an ethical responsibility to respect the worth and dignity of every individual who enters the healing space and whatever beliefs, world views, values, spiritual or religious beliefs, goals or desires they may hold.

For this reason and multiple others, a well-established awareness of self is imperative. The following points all relate broadly or specifically to the concept of self-awareness, which allows us to have knowledge of our own values and ethics and informs us of the judgements we may hold and the subtle and direct ways we can at times influence others.

Self-awareness ensures we are not persuading our clients to do what we think is right but rather have respect for the choices they make and their ability to determine what is right for their own lives. Further, self-reflection allows us the capacity to differentiate between what we know to be our own issues and what may be our clients' issues. We must always be aware of our own limitations and maintain professional boundaries.

When sensitive issues arise for clients who need ongoing or additional support it is essential that appropriate referrals are made to doctors, lawyers, financial advisers, counsellors, psychologists and so on. This involves us as healers having a real knowing of where our role ends and being respectful of our clients' right to follow their own path and learn their own lessons. We should never attempt to address issues for which we do not have professional training. Our intuition may pick up on issues for people, but it is very important to manage this in the most sensitive way and always refer to the most appropriate specialist service. Maintenance of our

professional boundaries is thus assured, always keeping in mind that for our clients it is their journey, their path to walk.

Self-care is vital in healing work. Our personal needs will always vary over time depending on what is happening for us at a given point, so this needs to be considered with flexibility. It is our responsibility to nurture ourselves with good physical health, nutrition, exercise and meditation and access reputable healthcare professionals when needed. Always remember to nurture yourself and your amazing gifts, because the more you nurture and cherish yourself the more you have within you to share with others.

Reference: Barbara Ann Brennan, 1988, *Healing Hands of Light: A guide to healing through the human energy field*, Bantam Books, New York.

THE THREE WORLDS OF SHAMANISM

CHAPTER 15

THE WORLDS

The three worlds of shamanism are the main non-reality worlds that shamans from all around the globe travel into to receive energy medicine and wisdom to assist in their healing and personal growth. The worlds have been accessed by shamans for thousands of years and exist in a different dimensional time and space. It's interesting to note that many different tribes journeyed to the worlds via similar practices even though they had no knowledge of each other's ways.

A range of allies, nature spirits and spirit beings reside on each of the lower, middle and upper worlds and each has its own specific energy and medicine. The worlds are universal and are available to access at will when you have an understanding of the sacred process. Once you are familiar with each world I will guide you through each one so you can experience them for yourself. We will journey to meet your power animal in the lower world, a crystal deva in the middle world and an angel or spirit guide who will bestow a blessing in the upper world.

CHAPTER 16

JOURNEYING TO THE THREE WORLDS

You can access the three worlds in a range of different ways; for example, via trance drumming, deep meditation or the dream state. In many traditions the worlds are accessed through sacred trees. The roots of trees are in the lower or inner world, the trunks are in the middle world and the branches are in the upper world, and they become a vortex and access point into the worlds. You can also enter by digging a hole in the earth or seeing yourself being lifted up by a hot air balloon, or any other way that you are guided to enter.

Drums and rattles have been used traditionally for thousands of years to support and assist people in entering a trance state and the worlds of shamanism. The drum or rattle is played in a constant fast, trance-like beat that balances the right and the left hemispheres of the brain. When your brain is in balance your heart opens and you can drop into a deep, meditative, trance-like state. The sound of the didgeridoo does a similar thing with its constant drone sound and vibration, guiding you into a deep, trance-like state.

Once you are in this state it is easier to access the worlds. You can also do the journey in silence or with meditation music. There are many trance drumming tracks available on the internet that you can use for your journey.

Once you are familiar with the three worlds you can travel at will to these sacred places; it is simply a matter of setting an intention. Make sure that once you are aware of your power animal you call upon them to facilitate your journeys into the three worlds, as they understand these worlds intimately.

It is a good idea to be in a very dark room for your journey, as this will help you drop into deep mediation and not get distracted by light. Your power animal always travels with you and will act as your guide.

The first thing to do before journeying into the three worlds is to set an intention about which world you would like to journey into or what your intention is for the journey. Once you are relaxed and have set your intention, call upon your power animal to take you on the journey. Visualise yourself travelling to your favourite tree and ask it if you can enter. If you are unable to get in through the tree, visualise yourself digging a hole or going up in a hot air balloon if you are travelling to the upper world. You will then enter the alternative reality of the world you have intended to travel to. Make sure your power animal is not following you into the worlds but that you are always following them, because if they are following you it means you are controlling the journey.

Once you arrive in the world you can travel around or just sit and wait to see what guide, spirit or ally meets you. The worlds look different for everyone, so make sure to trust and go with what's coming through for you. You will connect to the world through your senses, visualisations, feelings, hearing and knowing. Usually you will have a sense that is stronger than the others, so allow that one to guide you in your journeys. When you are in the world, surrender to the process and allow yourself to be guided.

Once you have received your medicine or met your guide, spirit, ally or power animal it will be time to return. To do this, visualise yourself going back in exactly the same way you got there. Take a moment to thank your allies and come back into the physical reality and your body. Make sure to work concisely with the medicine or guidance you received in your daily life to honour and respect the spirit of the medicine.

CRYSTALS TO ASSIST IN THE JOURNEY

There are several crystals that naturally hold the energy that will assist you to reach a trance state for your journey and unlock the doors to the three worlds. When you are travelling to the lower and middle worlds work with galena or Boji/shaman stones, as these crystals will anchor you in the physical plane and allow your spirit to know where to travel back to after the journey. When you're travelling to the upper world work with a higher-vibrational crystal such as selenite, which will open your crown chakra and connect you with the upper realms.

If you travel to the worlds for other people you will work with a clear quartz crystal as a tool to blow in the medicine. In this case the crystals will act as a transmitter of energy. When you use this technique it's important to be very present with the person and the medicine spirit. When you are in the world receiving the energy, medicine or soul fragment, make sure you gather the energy into your heart. When you come back from the worlds you will blow it into the heart and crown chakras of the person for whom you made the journey. In this process your heart becomes the vortex or conduit from the worlds into this physical reality, where you can then offer the medicine to another.

ASKING FOR CONFIRMATION

When you do your shamanic journey work it's a great idea to ask your guides, allies and spirit helpers to give you a clear sign as a confirmation of the medicine that was received in the process. For example, if you journeyed into the lower world and a snake came as your medicine you should receive three confirmations in the form of a snake once the journey has been completed. You may see a photo of a snake, someone might mention a snake or you may read about a snake or even hear lyrics of a song about a snake. The confirmations can come to you in a variety of ways; it's your job to be aware of them when they come. This process is a great way of building trust, clarity and confidence in your allies and in what you are receiving in your journeys.

IMPORTANT NOTE

It is essential to know that when you journey into any of the three worlds, and especially the lower world, there are energies that can travel back with you, so make sure before you return to brush off any cobwebs or debris. Also, when you are in the worlds don't take anything from anyone or anything that's not a part of the intention of your journey. You are travelling in these worlds with a certain intention, so be guided only by that intention.

If you are offered an item don't take it, as it could be an energy that wants to come back to the physical world. This is nothing to be scared of; however, similar to the physical reality, these are worlds of illusion and you do require a level of discernment. If you did bring something back you will need to cleanse and clear it from you by using a safe, powerful cleansing process. Please note that if you are journeying to receive a specific medicine in one of the worlds it is safe to bring that medicine back, as this was the intention of the journey.

It's a good idea to ask the guide, animal, ally or medicine spirit you met in the world to confirm three times who they are; if they are not who they appear to be they will go away. You shouldn't be frightened by the possibility of meeting an illusory guide as long as you understand these energetic safety requirements around journey work.

CHAPTER 17

THE LOWER (INNER) WORLD

The lower world is where your animal spirit totems and power animals reside and also where the wisdom of your ancestors is held. Similar to the earthly plane, this world can be one of illusion and magic so it is always a good idea to have a very strong, direct intent when you are travelling and only receive the medicine that shows up for that intention. For example, if you set an intention to travel for an animal guide then only receive that animal's medicine; don't take any other items that are offered.

You journey to the lower world by visualising yourself entering a hole in the earth or through the trunk of a tree and down into the earth itself.

Medicine that resides in the lower world: power animals, animal totems, allies and guides, wisdom and knowledge about your direct ancestors.

Crystals that will assist you on your journey: amber, Boji/shaman stones, chrysotile, galena, nuummite, petrified wood.

CRYSTAL ALLY

BOJI/SHAMAN STONES

Boji stones, also known as shaman stones, have been utilised by tribal people for thousands of years as guidance tools and healing gifts from the earth. These powerful allies assist in your journey into the worlds of spirit, where you connect to animal totems and many other gifts. They are great tools to work with in the soul-retrieval process as they allow for a shaman's energy to stay grounded in the earth plane. They bring about a balancing of the energy field when placed in your hands: the male stone in the left hand and the female in the right hand. This powerful alignment projects this medicine of balance into your life.

Boji stones:

- are powerful allies for shamans

- facilitate and assist shamanic and soul-retrieval journeys into the three worlds

- have deep connections with the medicine and wisdom of the earth

- awaken your inner shamanic power and wisdom

- help you to connect with your ancestors and their wisdom

- assist in releasing unwanted spirits and energetic attachments.

JOURNEYING TO THE LOWER WORLD

You are now going to journey into the lower world through a sacred tree or a hole in the earth to meet your power animal or animal totem or ally. On your journey more than one animal can show up for you, so make sure to ask it three times if it is your power animal or animal guide and if it remains after that then this is your confirmation. There can be times when more than one animal will stay after you have asked for confirmation, so if this happens work with all the animals that show up.

The crystal you will journey into the lower world with is galena or a shaman stone. This medicine is the key to open the lower world and will help keep you grounded in the physical while your spirit journeys.

PERSONAL HEALING

Make sure you follow the process for setting a sacred healing space as outlined in Chapter 13 before you begin this journey:

- Set your intention for your journey, in this case meeting your power animal or spirit guide. If you already know what your power animal is your journey will be slightly different, as you will journey to connect with another animal ally to help and guide you at this time. Make sure you set an intention on what guidance or healing you are after.

- Make sure you have something covering your eyes or you are in a dark room. Close your eyes and prepare yourself to journey, relaxing and bringing yourself into a centred space just as you do for meditation.

- Play trance drumming music.

- Take a few minutes to connect with your crystal and call in its deva to help you on your journey.

- Travel to your sacred tree or place in nature where there is an opening into the earth and journey down. Ask if you may enter into the tree, and if the answer is 'No' make your way down through another avenue.

- Travel down the opening into the lower world. Allow yourself to arrive, drop in and relax into the journey.

- It is time for your power animal to come to you. There could be several animals and beings that come to you in this place, so it's important you ask three times if an animal is your guide. If your animal is still there after you ask three times then this is your guide.

- Ask if you can merge your energy with your power animal's. Shapeshift into this energy and completely embody it. At this point your power animal may have a message for you.

⫷ Take as long as you feel comfortable in this space. When it feels as though the experience is done, thank your animal guide for the experience and return through your tree, brushing yourself off as you do so.

⫷ Come back into the physical reality and into your body in the here and now.

⫷ Thank your crystal deva.

Make sure you connect with your power animal on a regular basis just as you would with a friend to strengthen your bond and honour the connection.

Record your experience.

_____

_____

_____

_____

_____

_____

_____

_____

_____

_____

_____

_____

_____

_____

_____

_____

PRACTITIONER HEALING

When you journey for another person you will require a clear quartz crystal with a point, which you will use to blow in the medicine. Read through and familiarise yourself with the process before you offer it to another person. Also, make sure you follow the process for setting a sacred healing space as outlined in Chapter 13 before you offer healing to other people.

The intention of this journey can be to connect with your client's power animal or an animal for a specific healing. If it's a specific healing journey, connect with your client and ask what they are requiring healing for.

- Have your clear quartz crystal at hand to blow in the medicine.

- Take a moment to connect and call in the devas of your Boji/shaman stones or galena crystals.

- Make sure your client is sitting in a relaxed state and invite them to stay energetically open to receiving the medicine. Play trance drumming music and sit opposite your client with your knees touching.

- Set the intention to journey for your client's power animal or animal medicine that will assist in their healing.

- Set the intention that your client will get three solid confirmations from their power animal outside this healing space.

- Call upon your power animal and follow them into the lower world. Allow yourself to be guided by your power animal to meet your client's power animal or animal medicine. When they appear, take a moment to connect with your client's animal.

- Ask it three times if they are the correct medicine or power animal. If it remains it is the correct one, so ask if you can embrace it.

- Once you have embraced and embodied the energy in your heart, bring yourself back into the present and offer the energy to your client.

- Use the clear quartz crystal as a transmitter to blow in the energy.
- Your heart is the conduit from the inner world to the physical world.
- Draw the animal's energy from your heart and through your arms and hands, and blow into your client's crown chakra with a strong breath and then into their heart chakra. Make sure you are completely present when doing this process.
- Slowly bring your client back.
- Take some time to share with your client what power animal or medicine you received for them. Suggest they continue to connect with this energy every day to receive the full benefits of the journey.
- Let your client know they will get three confirmations of their animal in their day-to-day world.

Record your experience.

_____

_____

_____

_____

_____

_____

_____

_____

_____

_____

_____

CHAPTER 18

THE MIDDLE (PHYSICAL) WORLD

The middle world is the spiritual dimension of the physical world. It is here that you can connect with and become aware of the devas, allies or nature spirits of this world. Everything in nature has a soul and medicine to offer, and this is the world in which you travel to receive this energy. It is also where you travel to for soul retrieval and the healing of any old emotional or mental imbalances in your psyche. When you travel to this world it can feel a little congested as there is a great deal of psychic energy from human minds, but remember that you travel to these places to receive the positive energy only.

You journey to the middle world by visualising yourself stepping out of your body and travelling on the physical plane.

Medicine that resides in the middle world: the spirit of anything in the natural world, fairies, the moon and the sun, the spirits of the land, crystals and rocks, trees, plants and flowers, mountains, the ocean, stars, mental and emotional bodies.

Crystals that will assist you on your journey: agate, Apache tears, black obsidian, black tourmaline, bloodstone, carnelian, chrysocolla, cuprite, diopside, fluorite, garnet, hematite, jasper, jet, malachite, moonstone, pyrite, spirit quartz, sunstone.

CRYSTAL ALLY

AGATE

These are the benefits of agate as a crystal ally; it:

- restores, grounds and nurtures energy fields

- provides emotional and energetic support

- brings in all the divine qualities of Mother Earth

- reconnects you to the divine energy flow of the planet

- connects you deeply to Mother Earth and opens you to receive her powerful healing energy

- assists in shamanic journeying to meet the plant and tree devas.

JOURNEYING TO THE MIDDLE WORLD

You are now going to journey to the middle world to receive energy from an earth medicine, which you will do by allowing your spirit to leave your body and enter into the etheric realm of the physical plane. The energetic essence and spirit medicine of most things in the physical world reside in the middle world, and all of these different things can offer you guidance and healing; for example, you may travel to a flower, crystal, mountain, water, fire, earth, wind, plant or the sun or moon. You will also work with galena or shaman stones, as they help with access to the middle world as they do for the lower world.

PERSONAL HEALING

Your power animal will facilitate your trance drum journey to the middle world, so make sure you know what your power animal is before you start. If you don't know, make sure you undertake the meet your power animal journey in this book (see Chapter 4).

Make sure you follow the process for setting a sacred healing space as outlined in Chapter 13 before you begin this journey:

- Set your intention for your journey: what you would like to receive healing for.
- Cover your eyes or sit in a dark room.
- Close your eyes, relax and bring yourself into a centred space, just as you would for meditation.
- Play a trance drumming track and call in your power animal.
- Take a few minutes to connect with your crystal and call in its deva to help you on your journey.
- Trust your power animal and follow them as they guide you to your medicine, seeing your spirit rise from your body and travelling into the energetic space of the physical world. You could go to a flower, fire, mountain, the ocean, the clouds or anything that resides in the middle world.
- When you arrive at your medicine your power animal will gather it up and put it in a pouch around their heart.
- Come back with your power animal to your body in the physical plane. Take a moment to open and receive as your power animal blows the medicine into your crown chakra and then into your heart chakra.
- Spend a few minutes in this place.
- Thank your power animal, the medicine and your crystal.

≪ Come back into the present, bringing all aspects of self into the here and now.

You have been offered the medicine into your body and soul, so allow it to work its magic.

Record your experience.

_____

_____

_____

_____

_____

_____

_____

_____

_____

_____

_____

_____

_____

_____

_____

_____

_____

_____

_____

_____

PRACTITIONER HEALING

This process is exactly the same as when you do it for yourself, except this time you will journey with your power animal and you blow the medicine in for your client. When you journey for another person you need a clear quartz crystal with a point, which you will use to blow in the medicine. Also, make sure you follow the process for setting a sacred healing space as outlined in Chapter 13 before you offer healing to other people:

- Have your clear quartz crystal ready to assist you in blowing in the medicine.
- Ask your partner or client what they would like healing for.
- Take a moment to connect and call in the devas of your Boji/shaman stones or galena crystals.
- Make sure your client is sitting in a relaxed state and invite them to stay energetically open to receiving the medicine. Play trance drumming music and sit opposite your client with your knees touching.
- Set the intention to journey for a medicine for your client's healing and state your client's intention.
- Call on your power animal and follow them into the middle world.
- See your spirit rising from your body and travelling into the energetic space of the physical world.
- Trust your power animal and follow it as it guides you to your medicine. You could journey to a flower, fire, mountain, the ocean or the clouds.
- When you arrive at the medicine, gather it up and place it in your heart.
- Return to the physical plane and see the medicine move from your heart down to your arms and into your hands. Using the quartz crystal as a transmitter of the energy, blow the medicine into your client's crown chakra and then their heart chakra.

- ⫸ Spend a few minutes in this place.
- ⫸ Thank your power animal, the medicine and your crystal.
- ⫸ Guide your client back to the present and tell them to open their eyes.
- ⫸ Share what came through for you and any messages you may have for your client.

Record your experience.

_____
_____
_____
_____
_____
_____
_____
_____
_____
_____
_____
_____
_____
_____
_____
_____

CHAPTER 19

THE UPPER WORLD

The upper world is where the angels, ascended masters, spirit guides, light beings and high vibrational guides reside. It is a place of higher vibrational energy, is made of the divine light of the cosmos and is where deep wisdom and love are held.

You journey to the upper world by entering your tree and heading upwards or visualising yourself floating up to the heavens on a balloon, kite or bird or in any way you see yourself rising into the sky.

Medicine that resides in the upper world: spiritual teachers, angelic beings, masters, spirit guides, light beings, ascended masters, your higher self or 'I am' presence.

Crystals that will assist you on your journey: amethyst, celestite, danburite, labradorite, lapis lazuli, moldavite, pietersite, scolecite, selenite.

CRYSTAL ALLY

SELENITE

These are the benefits of selenite as a crystal ally; it:

⫷ is a powerful crystal that works like a vacuum cleaner to purify and cleanse your auric field

⫷ opens and stimulates your crown chakra and brings in the divine light of the cosmos, balancing your chakras

⫷ encourages you to take powerful action in your life

⫷ allows you to move forward in strength

⫷ connects to your higher self and 'I am' presence

⫷ shields your aura from any unwanted influences

⫷ detoxifies energy fields.

JOURNEYING TO THE UPPER WORLD

You are now going to experience the upper world, where all the higher vibrational beings reside. There you will meet a new spirit guide, ascended master or angel and receive a gift and some divine healing. This world will feel very different from the other two worlds: it will be a lot lighter in its essence. As with the lower and middle worlds you will access the upper world through your sacred tree, except this time you will head up into its branches. If you cannot enter through the tree for whatever reason then find an alternate way up.

The crystal ally you will connect with to enter the upper world is selenite, a magical crystal that opens up your crown chakra and assists you in aligning to the higher-vibration planes, thus it is perfect for this process.

PERSONAL HEALING

Make sure you follow the process for setting a sacred healing space as outlined in Chapter 13 before you begin this journey:

- ☀ Close your eyes, relax and bring yourself into a centred space, just as you would for meditation.
- ☀ Play a trance drumming track and call in your power animal for your journey.
- ☀ Take a few minutes to connect with your crystal and call in its deva to help you on your journey.
- ☀ Trust your power animal and follow it into the upper world.
- ☀ Go to your sacred tree or hop in your air balloon. If you are entering through your tree, ask for permission and make your way up into its branches.
- ☀ Allow yourself to arrive, drop in and relax into the journey as your angel, ascended master or new guide comes to you. They will offer you a healing, gift or message.
- ☀ Stay in this space as long as you feel comfortable as you receive the medicine from your new guide.
- ☀ When the experience has ended come back to the present, brushing yourself off as you come back through your tree.
- ☀ Thank your power animal, guide and the crystal deva for the experience.

Make sure you connect with your new guide on a regular basis just as you would with a friend to strengthen your bond.

Record your experience.

PRACTITIONER HEALING

When you journey for another person you need a clear quartz crystal with a point, which you will use to blow in the medicine. Also, make sure you follow the process for setting a sacred healing space as outlined in Chapter 13 before you offer healing to other people:

- Share with your client that you will be journeying for them to receive a gift and medicine from the upper realm.
- Take a moment to connect with and call in the deva of your selenite.
- Play trance drumming music and sit opposite your client with your knees touching. Invite your client to stay open energetically to receive the medicine.
- Set the intention to journey for a medicine or gift for your client.
- Close your eyes and prepare yourself to journey. Relax and bring yourself into a centred space.
- Call in your power animal for the journey and follow them to your sacred tree or jump into your air balloon. If you are entering through your tree, ask for permission to do so then make your way up into its branches.
- Your client's angel, ascended master or new guide will now come to you and offer you an energy or gift to take back for your client; receive this gift and place it in your heart.
- Thank the angel, ascended master or guide for the gift and head back to your tree and to the present moment, brushing yourself off as you do so.
- Thank your power animal and crystal deva.
- See the medicine move from your heart down your arms and into your hands. Using the clear quartz crystal as a transmitter of the energy, blow the medicine into your client's crown chakra and then into their heart chakra.

- Spend a few minutes in this place.
- Guide your client back to the present moment and guide them to slowly open their eyes.
- Share what came through for you and any messages you may have.

Record your experience.

_____

_____

_____

_____

_____

_____

_____

_____

_____

_____

_____

_____

_____

_____

_____

_____

_____

_____

_____

CHAPTER 20

MEDICINE RETRIEVAL JOURNEYING

Now that you know how to journey to each of the three worlds of shamanism you can travel any time you like. There is an abundance of medicine to receive in each of the worlds, so trust your power animal to guide you to the best medicine for you and your clients. All you need to do is set an intention for the journey and follow your power animal to any of the worlds. For example, your intention may be to receive healing to your leg, so you set this intention and follow your power animal to the lower, middle or upper world to receive the medicine they guide you to have. The two crystals you will work with are Boji/shaman stones and selenite.

Make sure you have journeyed to the lower, middle and upper worlds before you undertake a medicine retrieval journey, because it's important that you are familiar with the three worlds before you do so.

PERSONAL HEALING

Make sure you follow the process for setting a sacred healing space as outlined in Chapter 13 before you begin this journey:

- Put something over your eyes or situate yourself in a dark room.
- Set your intention for your journey, what you would like healing for.
- Play a trance drumming track.
- Close your eyes and prepare yourself to journey. Relax and bring yourself into a centred space, just as you would for meditation, and call in your power animal to guide your journey.
- Take a few minutes to connect with your crystals and call in their devas to help you on your journey.
- Allow yourself to be guided by your power animal and journey to either the lower world (for animal medicine), the middle world (for earth medicine) or the upper world (for a gift from light beings, angels or masters).
- When you become aware of the medicine being offered to you, embrace it and journey back with it to the physical plane.
- Spend a few minutes breathing the medicine into your heart, then send it through your body and into every single cell.
- Thank the medicine spirit, your power animal and the crystal devas.

Record your experience.

_____

_____

_____

PRACTITIONER HEALING

When you journey for another person you need a clear quartz crystal with a point, which you will use to blow in the medicine. Read through the process and familiarise yourself with it before you offer it to another person. Also, make sure you follow the process for setting a sacred healing space as outlined in Chapter 13 before you offer healing to other people:

- Connect with your client and ask what they are requiring healing for.
- Take a moment to connect with and call in the devas of your Boji/shaman stone or galena, agate and selenite. Have your clear quartz crystal ready to blow in the medicine.
- Play a trance drumming track and sit opposite your client with your knees touching.
- Set the intention to journey for a medicine that will assist in the healing of your client.
- Call upon your power animal and be guided by them as you journey to either the lower world (for animal medicine), the middle world (for earth medicine) or the upper world (for a gift from light beings, angels or masters).
- When you become aware of the medicine, embrace it and put it into your heart then journey back with it to the physical plane.
- Draw the medicine from your heart, and use the clear quartz crystal point to blow in energy to your client's heart and crown chakras.
- Share what came through for your client and any messages you may have.

Record your experience.

_____

_____

PART V

SHAMANIC HEALING PRACTICES

CHAPTER 21

PERSONAL POWER CRYSTAL

After years of becoming aware of and familiar with my power animal and what its medicine means to me I started to perceive that we must also have a power crystal: a crystal that resonates to the same frequency as our soul in this lifetime, an energy that holds the keys to our gifts and personal soul medicine. Although crystals constantly cross our paths and we attract them at the perfect time and space to share the medicine for what we need at that moment, I feel we also have one that truly resonates with our soul's vibration and stays with us and guides us throughout life.

Is it essential to know what your power crystal is? Not necessarily, but when you are aware of it you can work concisely with this energy to align yourself more to your own power, gifts and sacred personal medicine.

MY PERSONAL EXPERIENCE

I was offering the ceremony below to three women at a mind/body/ spirit expo in Tasmania. This event was an intimate gathering so I asked if the ladies would like to share their experience. The first lady shared that rose quartz had come through for her, the second lady also shared that rose quartz had shown up and then the third lady also said rose quartz had come to her. We were quite amazed by the realisation they had all received the same crystal and got their three confirmations even before they left the room. It was a powerful moment of recognition that this work is profound and tangible.

YOUR CEREMONY

The following ceremony will take you to meet your power crystal. Remember to ask for three confirmations that you have met the right crystal outside the meditation for clarity and a deeper connection and awareness. Note that you will also be working with a quartz crystal in this ceremony to assist you in connecting with the higher realms of the crystal kingdom. This can be any quartz crystal of your choice:

- While sitting in a quiet place, bring awareness to your breath and start to relax.
- Visualise yourself inside a six-pointed star made of light. This star is the *merkabah*, a cosmic vehicle in which you can travel to other realms.
- Imagine a six-pointed star around your crystal, then imagine another one around the earth.
- Take a moment to lock all three of the merkabahs together, then travel to the higher realms of the crystal kingdom.
- Be guided to your crystal temple, where you are welcomed by a beautiful crystal deva.
- You are invited to go inside the temple and sit on a throne in the centre of this sacred space.
- The temple's deva walks over to you and looks deeply into your eyes and soul, and invites you to hand over any fears or old beliefs that are holding you back from stepping into your power.
- Take a few moments to tune in to your mind, body and energy field, then gather up any of the belief systems, emotions and patterns that no longer serve you into a ball of light at your heart.
- Offer this light to the deva, who will then place the energy into their heart, transform it into power and love and hand it back to you.

- ⟨⟨ You are now invited to place this energy into your heart.

- ⟨⟨ The deva will place their hands upon your heart chakra and send the energy of your power crystal into it.

- ⟨⟨ Feel this energy permeate every cell of your being, activating your DNA and bathing your soul. Feel this medicine align you with your power and gifts in this life. This is your soul's medicine to awakening you to your 'I am' presence and best version of yourself.

- ⟨⟨ Stay in this space for a few minutes to receive this energy and blessing.

- ⟨⟨ The deva will share with you what your power crystal is and hand you a piece of it to place in your heart. Place your hands on your heart and know that this medicine is within you and is available at any time.

- ⟨⟨ The deva will offer you an inspirational message before you leave.

- ⟨⟨ Take a moment to say goodbye to the deva and thank them for your healing and guidance. The deva will always be with you to guide and support you.

- ⟨⟨ Imagine yourself coming back into your body.

- ⟨⟨ Unlock all three of the merkabahs and return to the present time and space.

- ⟨⟨ Call all aspects of self into the here and now and slowly open your eyes.

Now that you know what your power crystal is, make sure you actively work with its energy to assist you in stepping more completely into your power.

Record your experience.

_____

_____

_____

_____

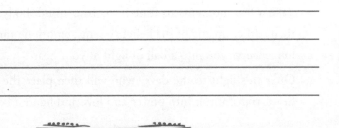

_____

_____

_____

_____

_____

_____

_____

_____

_____

_____

_____

_____

_____

_____

_____

_____

_____

_____

_____

_____

_____

_____

CHAPTER 22

SOUL RETRIEVAL

Have you ever had a challenging or traumatic event in your life that changed you and you never felt the same again? Throughout your life's journey you will experience numerous challenges and at times traumatic experiences and situations. The shock of these experiences can cause a rupture in your energy body and induce negative effects on your emotions and psyche as it traps the traumatic experience, creating a perceived disconnection from your soul. I personally don't believe this part gets completely severed from the soul body and that the trauma suppresses the positive aspect of the soul and lays dormant until that part is retrieved again and we release the negative energy that was suppressing it in the first place.

As a healer, with the support and guidance from your spirit team and power animal you can travel back to that time and place to retrieve the positive energy that was trapped due to the trauma. You can bring it back and align it to the present day, time and conciseness, awakening that part of the person's soul once again. We travel to the middle world to facilitate soul retrieval, as this is the world in which we can access the timelines of our lives.

I believe all healing is an act of soul retrieval, a process that invites you to embody more of your soul essence. 'Healing' means discovering how perfectly whole and complete you already are, remembering your divine essence and discarding any beliefs that keep you from knowing and experiencing your divinity. At the core, healing occurs when your mind, body and spirit are aligned with their true authentic selves.

Soul retrieval can be practised in many ways and using an abundance of different processes. I shared a story at the start of the book about travelling to Sedona to retrieve a piece of my heart that I had left there in another lifetime. I had the rare opportunity of physically travelling to a location to retrieve that soul part, although most soul retrieval is done energetically.

The majority of the healing processes I teach involve the client being an active part of the healing process, as I believe it to be extremely empowering for them. However, there will be times when you need to facilitate the whole healing for your client to show them the way until they feel strong enough to take the wheel.

BEFORE UNDERTAKING A SOUL RETRIEVAL JOURNEY

Sometimes when you journey for your client you will know exactly what aspect you are bringing back for them and at other times you may not. Don't get attached to knowing what it may be as it's more important to be present to the energy that shows up, to trust and work with what shows itself. If your client is meant to know what the fragment is then you will know, and if they are not meant to know it will not be shown to you. It can be a more powerful experience not knowing and just trusting in the energy.

The first time I facilitated this type of soul retrieval I had no idea what I was doing and really had to trust in the process. Once I let go and went with it a very powerful healing was offered. I will share the story below in my personal experience, but for now I invite you to set the same intention and trust your power animal and the process in this journey. Don't judge yourself in the process or believe the message you received doesn't mean anything or that you're no good at soul retrieval. Set your intention, trust your power animal and honour whatever comes through. If you truly

are not getting anything, be honest with your client and let them know. It could possibly be that they may not be ready or their guides won't allow the process at this time. Trust and know that it is all in divine order.

MY PERSONAL EXPERIENCE

I would like to share a very special experience I had with Steven Farmer in 2004 that highlights the potency of this type of soul retrieval and why I teach this work today. Steven, Doreen Virtue's former husband, took us through a powerful soul retrieval at one of Doreen's advanced workshops. I had never experienced one in this format before and had no idea what I was doing, but I trusted the process and followed Steven's guidance.

There would have been more than 600 people in the room, and we were invited to pair up with someone we didn't know. I connected with a lovely lady with whom I am still friends. One person in the process would be the shaman and would journey for the other person. We decided that I would be the shaman first and we sat facing each other with our knees touching. Steven then asked us to call in our power animals to support the journey. I didn't know what mine was at the time, so I called on my spirit guides to assist me.

A group intention was set to travel into the middle world to retrieve an aspect of the person's soul that had been fragmented due to some form of trauma, then bring the energy back and blow it into the crown and heart chakras. As Steven played the trance drum beat I closed my eyes and followed my intuition into the middle world, and I immediately found myself in an old hospital with grey walls and stale energy. I was under a baby's humidicrib and could see a bright light in the top right corner of the crib, and I knew without a doubt that this was what I was there to retrieve.

I reached out and grabbed it and brought it back into my physical body and heart.

From that place I offered the energy to my partner and blew it into her crown and heart chakras, and as she received the energy she started to sob. I held the space while she processed what she had received and then shared with her what I had seen and experienced. She looked at me and

said, 'I was adopted at birth,' so what we had retrieved was the part of her soul that had remained in the hospital. It was a very profound and sacred experience: she hadn't realised how much her adoption had affected her until she got the soul fragment back, and now she feels complete.

This experience was incredibly humbling for me, as it had been so simple yet powerful. Setting the intention and journeying to the middle world for the retrieval brought about so much healing, and I would like to give full honour and respect to Steven and his lineage for offering me this experience so I could understand it and then embody my own style of soul retrieval and teach it to others.

PERSONAL HEALING

Work with Boji/shaman stones or galena in this ceremony. Your power animal will guide the journey for you, and once the soul energy or fragment has been retrieved they will blow it into your crown and heart chakras. All you need to do is set the intention and give permission to your power animal to retrieve the aspect of your soul that has been suppressed due to trauma, then open and receive the healing.

Make sure you follow the process for setting a sacred healing space as outlined in Chapter 13 before you begin this journey. You can choose a specific issue to retrieve or you can leave the process in the hands of spirit:

⋘ Take a moment to connect with and call in the deva of your Boji/shaman stone or galena or agate crystal and play some drumming music. Have your clear quartz crystal ready to blow in the medicine.

⋘ Call in your power animal and set the intention that they journey to receive an aspect of your soul that was suppressed due to trauma.

⋘ Your power animal will now journey to the middle world (the spiritual aspect of the physical plane) to retrieve the energy.

⋘ Set an intention to stay open to receive whatever comes when your power animal returns with the soul fragment and blows it into your crown and heart chakras.

⋘ Stay in this energy for as long as you like while you integrate the energy.

⋘ Thank your power animal and crystal devas.

Record your experience.

_____

_____

PRACTITIONER HEALING

The process below has been utilised for thousands of years by shamans, and as you will be facilitating the healing for another person it's important to know that when you undertake soul retrieval you are retrieving positive energy that was left in a particular time and place. As you bring it back and blow the energy into your client's soul it will dissolve the negative energy that was creating the suppression, so that part of their soul can realign with them in the present time and space reality. Whenever you blow anything into someone else you need to be completely present to the process and working from a place of love.

Before you take someone else on this journey please ensure you are familiar with and have had journeys in all three worlds and that you have been through a soul retrieval of your own with your power animal. Also, make sure you follow the process for setting a sacred healing space as outlined in Chapter 13 before you offer healing to other people:

⋘ Connect with your client and set an intention to journey for a part of your client's soul that has been fragmented in time and space due to a form of trauma. You can choose a specific issue to retrieve or you can leave the process in the hands of spirit.

⋘ Take a moment to connect with and call in the devas of your Boji/shaman stone or galena or agate crystal. Have your clear quartz crystal ready to blow in the medicine.

⋘ Play drumming music and sit opposite your client with your knees touching.

⋘ Call upon your animal spirit guides and follow them on the journey to the middle world (the spiritual aspect of the physical plane). You might or might not get a clear vision or knowing of where you are going and how it relates to your client. The most important things are setting the intention, trusting and bringing back the energy that presents itself.

- When you arrive in the time and space of the soul fragment, embrace it, place it in your heart and return with it.
- Draw the soul fragment from your heart and use your quartz crystal point to blow in and offer energy into your client's heart and crown chakras.
- Take some time to sit with your client as they receive this soul energy.
- Call them back energetically into their bodies and into the current time and space.
- Thank your power animal and crystal devas and share whatever you experienced with your client.

Record your experience.

_____

_____

_____

_____

_____

_____

_____

_____

_____

_____

_____

_____

_____

_____

_____

CHAPTER 23

SHAPESHIFTING

Shapeshifting is a very powerful and sacred union that is created with the soul and spirit of a power animal or earth medicine. It is found in almost all shamanic cultures and is usually kept as a secret healing process due to its immense power. Shapeshifting is the practice of completely embodying the energy and spirit of an animal, crystal, ocean, mountain or anything you feel a calling to connect with in nature. In the shapeshifting process you metamorphose into an alternative reality in which you align with the interconnectedness of all that is and the soul of the chosen medicine. You enter into the web of life and call upon the spirit of the medicine to fully embrace you as you embody and become this energy in every cell of your being, then shapeshift back into the physical world as a physical manifestation of that medicine, ally or spirit being.

There are many ways to shapeshift, and of course intention is a big part of the process. To connect deeply with something you need to find a common energy system you both share, and in this process it is the chakras. You will align your chakras together and fully immerse yourself in the energy and spirit of the other being.

Shapeshifting allows you to have a direct experience with the chosen medicine's spirit and consciousness. It is a very sacred and intimate process in which you will understand what it feels like to be the actual medicine, animal or being you are shifting into. You will receive a direct knowing and embody the wisdom from the experience. Once you have shapeshifted it is extremely important to continue working with the medicine as a sacred honouring, creating a soul contract with the spirit. You will know when it's time to stop connecting with the ally as you will get a strong sense that your work together is done.

The following are reasons why you might shapeshift:

- To seek and embody the qualities from a specific medicine to receive healing and wisdom.
- It's an important part of the spiritual path and a much-required tool of growth in attaining wisdom and healing.
- It's a powerful process that will allow you to deepen your connection with your spirit allies.

BEFORE SHAPESHIFTING

Read through and understand these things before you undertake a shapeshifting journey:

- Shapeshifting is an advanced process that requires full commitment, surrender, trust and practice to master.
- It is a very sacred practice and requires to be treated as such.
- Allow yourself to go beyond your ego mind.
- Always ask permission of the allies or spirits you intend to shapeshift with.
- You will be activating and using the chakra energy system to connect. You will connect your chakras with the chakras of your chosen ally, spirit or object.
- The main focus will be on the solar plexus chakra.
- You will completely embody your chosen animal, ally or spirit.

- Shapeshifting occurs in ordinary and non-ordinary states of being; there is full embodiment in the spiritual and physical worlds at the same time.

- Most shapeshifting journeys occur in the middle world.

MY PERSONAL EXPERIENCE

The following story highlights the power of shapeshifting and animal medicine all in one. I was chilling on the bed with a friend and having a lazy day. She was writing and I was playing with my dog, Gaia. She leaned over and started drawing something on the back of my neck, which invoked a very powerful experience for me. I started to zone out, and within seconds I had shapeshifted into a redback spider. It may sound crazy but it definitely happened, and I can still remember to this day how it felt. I experienced an incredible energy of feminine power and could see hundreds of baby spiders in my web that I would do anything to protect. The experience only lasted about 10 seconds; however, it will stay with me forever.

When I came out of it I said: 'You wouldn't believe what just happened, but I just shapeshifted into a spider.' She then told me that she had drawn a heart on the back of my neck over an old spider bite I have, which had invoked the experience. She offered to look up in the animal medicine book what it meant but I told her I didn't need that as I knew with every cell of my being what it was like to be a spider.

Around this time I was gifted a piece of chrysotile, which I later came to understand is a huge ally in connecting us with our animal spirit medicine. There was no mistake that this beautiful piece naturally had my power animal etched into it, which for me was further confirmation: I feel as though this shapeshifting experience allowed me to embody the full energy of this medicine within myself. For me the spider medicine was related to my spiritual business, as I created a spiritual web with my workshops and people came into the web to be inspired and empowered and would then take this healing energy out into the world.

Over time as I integrated the spider medicine I felt it had a big impact on my teachings and was another inspiration for me to create my crystal

shaman workshops. It is no surprise that I have been bitten by many spiders in my life and specifically by redback spiders. I did become ill when bitten but I was young and healthy and quickly bounded back. When a spider bites you it is offering its medicine to you in the physical realm, and receiving it can be an intense and sacred rite of passage. Over the years spiders have offered me their potent medicine just at the right time for me to use this energy to embody my creative gifts and enhance my teachings and path of helping others.

Six weeks after the shapeshifting experience I spoke at a mind/body/spirit expo in Sydney. After I finished I walked down into the festival and saw right in front of me a stand named 'Red Spider Woman'. I saw an Elder sitting on a chair and felt a strong pull to go and meet her. After I had introduced myself and she shared with me that she was Red Spider Woman, one of the Counsel of 13 Grandmothers, medicine women who travel the globe sharing ancient ceremonies and the medicine of the old ways. Their message is to invite a marrying of the old and new ways so we can all work in harmony for the greater good of humanity. I sat with her as we shared stories and received many confirmations of my shapeshifting experience. This Elder gave me clarity on many things that were occurring in my life.

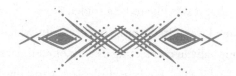

YOUR CEREMONY: SHAPESHIFTING INTO A CRYSTAL

You would shapeshift into a crystal if you wanted to create a deep union and connection with this medicine. Choose what crystal you would like to shapeshift into, then:

- Play trance drumming music.
- Get comfortable, close your eyes and drop into a relaxed state of being. You will travel into the middle world for this journey.
- Call to the spirit or deva of the crystal you would like to shapeshift with.
- Allow yourself to be guided to wherever it may be residing then, once you arrive, ask it for its sacred name. If the name is given to you then you have permission to shapeshift into that crystal.
- Set a strong intention for shapeshifting and healing.
- Focus on your solar plexus with the intention of turning it on. See, feel or imagine the solar plexus chakra of the crystal deva, then join your solar plexus with the crystal's solar plexus.
- Starting at the base chakra, link all of your chakras one by one with the chakras of the crystal deva, repeating the crystal's name throughout the process.
- Once all your chakras are aligned you can merge as one with your crystal.
- Stay there for as long as you feel drawn to.
- Once the process is finished, unlock all your chakras, thank the crystal deva and return to your body.

Make sure you continue to work consciously with the spirit of the crystal and the medicine.

Record your experience.

_____

_____

_____

_____

_____

_____

_____

_____

_____

_____

_____

_____

_____

_____

_____

_____

_____

_____

_____

_____

_____

YOUR CEREMONY: SHAPESHIFTING INTO AN ANIMAL GUIDE OR ALLY

You would shapeshift into an animal guide or ally if you wanted to create a deep connection with this medicine. You can undertake this journey with trance drumming or other music or in silence. Choose what animal guide or ally you would like to shapeshift into, then:

- Tune in to their spirit and ask for their permission to shapeshift. If you feel a sense of openness and lightness you have permission, but if you feel any blockage or doubt then you don't have permission and you can try again another time or choose a different medicine.

- Allow yourself to be completely present and clearly state your intention to shapeshift, then journey to the non-reality middle world.

- Call upon your animal guide or ally, seeing and sensing them clearly in front of you.

- Focus your attention on your solar plexus and activate it, then align your solar plexus energy with the solar plexus of your animal guide.

- Starting at the base, link all of your chakras one by one with the chakras of your animal guide or ally. Make sure your full attention and focus is on what you are doing.

- Once your chakras are aligned fully, emerge and shapeshift into the medicine. Stay there for as long as you are guided to.

- Once the process is finished, unlock all your chakras, thank the spirit and return to your body.

Make sure you continue to work consciously with the spirit of the animal guide or ally and the medicine.

Record your experience.

_____

_____

_____

_____

_____

_____

_____

_____

_____

_____

_____

_____

_____

_____

_____

_____

_____

_____

_____

_____

_____

YOUR CEREMONY: SHAPESHIFTING INTO THE OCEAN

Shapeshifting into the ocean will allow you to embody the qualities of water. You don't have to be physically at the ocean, but if you can be it would enhance the process. You can undertake this journey with trance drumming or other music or in silence.

- Before you journey, contact the spirit of the ocean to ask for its permission.
- Sense into the spirit of the ocean and ask if it is okay to shapeshift. If you feel a sense of openness and lightness then you have permission, but if you feel any blockage or doubt then you don't have permission and you can try again another time or choose a different medicine.
- Lie down and relax, surrender and trust. Allow yourself to be completely present.
- Clearly state your intention to shapeshift into the ocean, then call upon your power animal and follow it into the middle world to meet the spirit of the ocean.
- Once you arrive, take a moment to deeply connect with the ocean.
- Put your complete focus on shapeshifting into the water and take a moment to align all of your chakras with the chakras of the water.
- Surrender and allow the ocean to merge with you; you will become one with the ocean.
- Stay there for as long as you feel comfortable doing so.
- When it is time to return, detach your chakras, thank the ocean spirit and return to your body.

Make sure you continue to work consciously with the spirit of the ocean and the medicine it offered you.

Record your experience.

_____

_____

_____

_____

_____

_____

_____

_____

_____

_____

_____

_____

_____

_____

_____

_____

_____

_____

_____

CHAPTER 24

THE SHADOW SELF

'Shadow self' is the term used to explain the aspects of our personality that we hide and run from, that we deny, judge, fear and disassociate with. It contains all of the emotions that have been suppressed over the years due to misunderstanding, judgement and trauma, all of the parts of us that we are scared of, uncomfortable with or ashamed of that we have denied and shut ourselves off from due to some form of fear. Throughout life we share different parts of ourselves with other people and at times we get hurt, then we tend to push these traits and feelings into the unconscious or the shadow and close down these parts of ourselves.

All perceived positive and negative traits can be held in the shadow self; for example, if you have been hurt in love you can shut down that part of yourself and place it in the shadow. Working on your shadow or unconscious self can seem very scary when in truth it can be one of the most rewarding and life-enhancing processes you can ever undertake, as it's how you learn and grow and empower yourself to live your most authentic life. It's a road to freedom and nowhere near as frightening as it

sounds, and although it may be a little uncomfortable it is certainly worth the challenge.

The journey to uncover your shadow self is a very sacred and powerful one that contains great personal power, strength and an abundance of healing. As you bring awareness and love to what's held in your shadow you can gently invite those parts of yourself to come out of the dark and into the light, and in the process you will come more into your fullness, totality and truth and start to love and respect all of who you are.

Life on earth exists within the law of polarity: night and day, up and down, the sun and the moon, hot and cold, happy and sad. Both light and dark exist within everything. As above so below, within and without, and you have all aspects that exist within you. Polarity allows you to experience the different aspects of things and is how you learn and grow. Within every cell of your being is all the wisdom of the universe, light and dark and everything in between. We all come from the same source and are connected to all that is.

When you deny or suppress emotions they get pushed into the shadow or unconscious where you can't see them. They then play havoc with your life and you project your negative thoughts and feelings onto other people. You then blame, point the finger and judge this behaviour in the people around you and deny it within yourself. This is called projecting. You start to see these traits in others because it is easier to see them in someone else than it is to see them in yourself.

You are a mirror, and you couldn't see something in someone else if it was not also in you. A powerful key and tool to highlight what you are holding in the shadow is when you get emotionally triggered. When someone says or does something that makes your blood boil and you get defensive you have been emotionally triggered, and it can highlight something you are denying in yourself.

Whenever you find yourself pointing the finger, blaming or projecting, take some time to drop into what it is inside you that you are reacting to. It's something that is held in your shadow self, something you don't love that you judge or deny. Once you know what it is you can carry out inner work, being brutally honest with yourself in self-reflection, acceptance, love and kindness that will bring this aspect back into the light and into

your awareness. This will enable you to take back your power, to set yourself free from old wounds, beliefs and patterns.

Whenever you blame and point the finger you are handing your power over to that person, whereas being honest with yourself and working with the shadow and owning these behaviours, emotions and traits will bring the power back to you so you can make positive change.

Connecting with and embracing your shadow self is about being kind to yourself and accepting and loving all of the parts of you. Bringing negative emotions out of your unconscious and into your conscious will give you power over them. You have the choice of behaving in a positive manner instead of playing out your life in denial and projection. When you have the courage and strength to face this darkness, to go within and sit with fear, you will soon experience and understand that your power and an abundance of wisdom and gifts are hidden within this place. Your biggest fears and the things you hold in your shadow are your greatest gifts, and when you have the courage to bring them out into the light you will receive the blessings they offer.

I wish to share a great analogy with you that sums up the shadow self perfectly. You were born into a huge mansion that has in it every trait and aspect within the universe: love, creativity, passion, fear, jealousy, joy, anger, disappointment, rage, abandonment, jealously and so on. As life goes on you invite people into your different rooms. For example, you may invite someone into your creativity room and show them a drawing you created or sing them a song, or into your joy room where you express your glee. If they reject what you have shown or done for them you will close those doors and lock them, or in other words you close down those parts of yourself. You go through life inviting many people into these different rooms and showing people these different aspects of yourself. You get rejected and hurt and start to lock all the doors in your mansion, and eventually you end up living in a one-bedroom flat!

The wonderful thing is that these rooms never disappear and you have the ability to unlock the doors whenever you choose to; you just need understanding, kindness, love and compassion. The work of the shadow self is to bring the hidden parts of yourself into the light and love all of you so you can live a life of choice, empowerment, freedom and totality.

To sum up, denying your shadow self creates mental and emotional imbalance, which in turn creates depression and addiction; you are meant to experience all human emotions without judgement, as this is how you learn and expand. By owning and accepting your shadow self you can connect and align with your true power and magnificence. A shaman understands this deeply and works with both the light and dark and fully accepts these aspects in balance. Light and dark is all energy, and it is your judgement of positive and negative that gives energy its charge. Energy is simply energy!

I would like to share a great idea that nicely sums up the shadow self. If you never journeyed outside into the darkness at night you would never see the magnificence of the stars and the moon and their magical light. The same applies to you: if you don't delve into your shadow self you don't get to experience your magnificence to its full potential.

MY PERSONAL EXPERIENCE

The journey of awakening the shadow self is definitely a lifelong commitment, and for me my deepest shadow shows up in my love life. Intimate relationships are one of my biggest challenges, but the bigger the challenge the bigger the blessing! Because of the wounds I had around my father I had closed off my heart and placed walls around it so I couldn't get hurt. Most relationship issues arose due to the unresolved pain from my father.

I attracted romantic partners that didn't treat me very well as this was what I thought I deserved. As I started to heal the wounds around my dad and do some deep inner work I attracted a different partner into my life, one who was more understanding and loved me unconditionally. As my old beliefs and patterns started to shift and I became more open to receiving love I thought the relationship was everything I'd ever wanted, but there was a part of me that couldn't accept it. I acted out and was starting to realise at times I was mean to my partner. At first I denied this part of myself, as I had never really seen myself as a mean person, then I realised that in the past I had justified my not so nice behaviour as I was in relationships with people who were nasty to me. However, this behaviour just kept me in the cycle.

The reflection I was now seeing in the mirror in my relationship was one of love, and I didn't know what to do with it. Then I had a profound awareness and opening: for me to shift this behaviour from my shadow self and release myself from the cycle I first had to surrender to it. I had to be truthful with myself and stop blaming other people, and I had to acknowledge the behaviour and be honest about the fact that I could be nasty when I felt threatened. Once I surrendered to this truth I was able to drop deeper into it, and I came to realise why I felt I had to be mean: so I could push people away so I didn't have to open my heart and be vulnerable and in a position to get hurt again.

I cried and cried when I had the realisation and understood the judgement I had placed on myself. This awareness allowed this trait to come out of the dark and into the light, from my unconscious into my conscious awareness. The love and acceptance gave me an opportunity to shift an old pattern and hold myself in kindness and compassion. If I hadn't accepted this aspect of myself and continued to blame, deny and beat myself up for it I would never have created an opportunity to shift it. The meanie part of me is still there, but I have the power to choose my behaviour in the future in the face of love.

CRYSTAL ALLIES

Many crystals can assist you to connect with and embrace your shadow side. Each of the following crystals brings awareness and light to the parts of yourself you hide away from or deny, and each has a unique energy and works in a slightly different way. The best way to connect with these crystals is to have your own experience so that you integrate and embody the medicine for yourself, invoking your own individual healing and awakening.

Awakening crystal (elestial quartz): clears and brings balance to your emotional body; helps to navigate negative reactions when you are emotionally triggered; soothes your nervous system; and supports the healing process of addiction.

Black amethyst: balances light and dark; helps you to see into the darkness with clarity; heals any wounds held in the darkness; and assists you to let go of shame and guilt.

Black calcite: helps to manage anxiety and depression; brings calmness to chaos; and soothes emotional pain.

Black moonstone: brings light to the unseen parts of yourself; opens the door to your inner realms; supports you when you drop into the void of your shadow self; and deeply connects you with the feminine part of your psyche.

Black obsidian: is a powerful cleanser of negative energy in your body and energy field; places a protective shield over your auric field; and grounds you into the heart of the earth.

Black tourmaline: transmutes lower or negative energies; strengthens and protects your aura, allowing you to feel safe in your own energy field; and is grounding and holds a very powerful clearing energy.

Cuprite: assists you to explore your shadow self, healing deep issues related to the sacred feminine as you are supported to enter into your own personal healing cave for self-reflection; gives access to sacred ancient knowledge of the feminine and is used for rites of passage; and supports and holds you as you enter into the void of the shadow, a journey that is necessary for deep transformational healing.

Jet: assists you in entering into the void of your shadow self, where you obtain your true depth of self-understanding and power; clears and protects your energy field and aura; and stimulates the awakening of kundalini energy.

Nuummite: supports you on the journey into your shadow self, allowing a sacred space to obtain deep wisdom, strength and courage; assists you on the journey of self-mastery; and helps you to love all aspects of yourself.

Shungite: allows you to deeply connect with your shadow side and receive the gifts it has to offer; balances, protects and grounds you; allows for self-reflection; and releases painful, deep-seated negative behaviour patterns and beliefs.

YOUR HEALING

This powerful ceremony will enable you to meet your shadow self and start being aware of those aspects of yourself you may be denying or suppressing. Make sure to work with one of the shadow crystals listed above to assist in the process:

⋙ Put on some relaxation music, close your eyes and imagine yourself at the edge of a sacred forest.

⋙ You are invited to journey deep into this beautiful forest, where you are surrounded by nature.

⋙ As you walk in the magical forest, be aware of Mother Earth under your feet and feel your connection with her as you journey deeper and deeper into the forest.

⋙ Become aware of the nature spirits and the spirits of this sacred land, and take a moment to honour these friends of the forest. Feel their love and healing as they welcome you to this sacred land and feel the energy and spirits of the trees.

⋙ As your heart expands, breathe in the nurturing healing energy to every cell of your being.

⋙ Allow yourself to be bathed in the essence of this sacred forest and open your heart to receive the blessings.

⋙ Journey even deeper into the heart of the forest and become aware of an ancient tree, the guardian of this land. Take a few moments to connect with the tree.

⋙ Sit down with your back against the tree, becoming aware of a presence and energy that is rising from under the tree and into the trunk and then into your heart.

⋙ Feel it move from your heart and manifest in front of you: this is your shadow self. Connect with it for a moment, how it looks and feels and its shape and colour.

⋙ Ask your shadow self what aspects are held here: old beliefs, patterns and fears.

⋙ Think about what you would like to say to your shadow self and what your shadow self would like to say to you. Take a few minutes to share these thoughts.

⋙ Sense a bright light energy travelling down from the heavens and into the branches of the tree, then into its trunk and into your heart and manifesting in front of you: this is your higher self, which has come to facilitate your healing.

❧ All three aspects of you now gather in this sacred space: your shadow self, your higher self and your current self. Be a witness while your shadow self hands over to your higher self any fears, traumas and old belief systems that no longer serve.

❧ Witness your higher self transmute these fears into courage, power, strength, love, acceptance and compassion.

❧ Your higher self now offers you a key of love to open when the time is right any other doors that have been locked.

❧ Place the key in your heart, knowing you now have the tools of transformation and freedom.

❧ Your higher self and shadow self now merge as one.

❧ Breathe both these aspects of yourself into your heart as you fully integrate these two powerful parts.

❧ Stay in this space for as long as you feel comfortable doing so.

❧ When you return to the present, thank Mother Earth, the nature spirits, your crystal's deva and your higher self.

Record your experience.

_____

_____

_____

_____

_____

_____

_____

_____

_____

_____

INTEGRATING SHADOW-SELF HEALING

The powerful layout below will deeply assist to work with your shadow aspects. You will connect with and receive the medicine of black obsidian, which will draw suppressed energies to the surface, and black tourmaline, which helps to clear suppressed energies from the field like a huge universal vacuum so you can bring this energy back into balance within you.

In this healing you will also deeply connect with your breathing. It's important to take long, deep belly breaths, as your breath can switch on and amplify crystal medicine. In addition, when you breathe in this way it will allow all of the cells of your body to open and expand so you can more fully receive the energy of the crystals. As you breathe deeply the golden light of the universe will pulse through you, which will also amplify the process.

In this healing you will be working with a Star of David formation, a very sacred geometry that has been found on many ancient sites around the globe. This is the shape of the merkabah, your light body that holds your soul in your physical body. It is the cosmic vehicle you travel in to alternative dimensions and higher realms. You will infuse the crystal medicine into your light body and shower it through your spiritual, emotional and mental bodies into your physical body so your whole being gets infused with the energy.

You can carry out this healing on yourself or you can guide someone else through it. Make sure to call in the devas of the tourmaline and black obsidian crystals to assist you in the activation. Place one black tourmaline crystal and one obsidian crystal at each point indicated on the diagram and on each chakra and both of your hands.

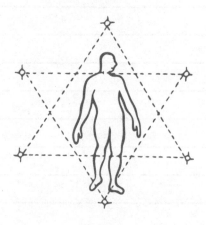

For the first four minutes, breathe deeply and visualise the following:

- On your in breath, activate and breathe the golden light of the universe down through your crown chakra and into your physical body. Breathe this light into every cell of your being, then send it down and out the bottom of your feet to anchor it into the earth.
- On your out breath, breathe this light through every pore of your skin, into your aura and into the crystals that lay upon and around you. This light will activate the crystals as they amplify their energy.
- On your next in breath, breathe the crystals' energy back into your body, into every cell and into your heart.
- On your next out breath, send the energy back into your aura.
- Continue breathing deeply for four minutes, amplifying the crystals' energy with every breath you take.

For the last four minutes:

- Allow your breathing to find its natural flow.
- Relax and see yourself being bathed by this medicine.
- When you are finished, thank the devas of the crystals.

Record your experience.

_____

_____

_____

_____

_____

_____

_____

_____

CHAPTER 25

MEDICINE EARTH WALK

Mother Earth and her spirit allies have guided and taught the shamans and medicine people of the world from the beginning of time, and the connection is one that runs deep within the heart and soul. A powerful way to strengthen this union is by taking a medicine walk, which is a sacred walk upon the earth that allows you to become open and sensitive to the medicine that is being offered and enhances your connection to nature. By taking the time to slow down and walk slowly and gently on the land and become present in nature you will feel more at one with this sacred space, and your ability to receive messages and signs from the medicines of the earth will become a lot stronger and clearer.

You would embark upon an earth walk if you required medicine for healing or an answer to a personal challenge or problem in your life. Everything in nature has a soul and medicine to share with us; the medicine will cross your path at the perfect time for what you need at that particular

point in your life. When you slow down and take the time to be present to your surroundings you will become more aware of what is interacting with you and the energy or message it has to offer.

This deep connection and this ritual have been forgotten in today's world, and most people run through life missing the signs and energy that is offered to them. The great expression that says to remember to stop and smell the roses explains this to a tee. In many cultures, when a person went on a walkabout it was to receive the wisdom that was needed, and most times this was found in nature.

There are several steps to follow when embarking upon your earth medicine walk:

⋘ It's important to set an intention before you go on your earth walk. Sit quietly with your eyes closed and clearly set your intention. It could be a question about anything in your life or asking for guidance or healing.

⋘ Call forth the nature medicine by offering some sort of song or energy; you can play a drum, rattle, crystal bowl or bells or sing a song. This is an honouring and calling for the medicine to show itself.

⋘ When you feel guided to, take your walk in nature. Make sure you walk slowly and gently upon the earth and be as present as you can be.

⋘ Become aware of anything that may be attracting your attention. It could be a feather or leaf being blown by the wind, a branch of a tree moving or the sun shining on something – anything that takes your attention.

⋘ When you know what is calling you, walk over and sit with the medicine. Spend as much time there as you like as you commune with the spirit of the medicine. See what it has to share with you about your question: how do you feel when you're with it, and what insights come to you? You may receive visualisations, thoughts, feelings or knowings.

⋘ Once you have received your clarity, healing or medicine, take some time to offer a song, prayer, piece of hair or any other gift as an offering of gratitude and thanks.

⋘ Come back to your natural state of being.

If the experience didn't feel as intense as you might have imagined it would be, know that sometimes the awareness comes after the walk. Also know that whatever you receive is perfect and is working on many levels.

Record your experience.

_____

_____

_____

_____

_____

_____

_____

_____

_____

_____

_____

_____

_____

_____

_____

_____

_____

_____

_____

_____

_____

CHAPTER 26

PERSONAL SPIRITUAL ALTAR

Altars are a physical manifestation of a certain intention; they hold sacred space and are a tool of great respect and honour. You can create altars for a vast range of intentions such as abundance, healing, honouring ancestors and for a deeper connection with people, places and things. The process described below for creating a personal spiritual altar will help you to ground the energy of your spiritual practice into your physical reality, keeping your spiritual practice alive and giving you something tangible to focus on. Most of your spiritual connection happens in the unseen realms, and creating a spiritual altar will invoke the energy into the physical plane and infuse it into your day-to-day life. As you tend to your altar and give it energy, it will then tend and nurture your spiritual connection.

Altars bring positive, fresh energy into your life. A good place to set up your altar is somewhere in which you spend a lot of your time, in a peaceful

environment where you are able to see it regularly. Collect sacred items to place on your altar such as:

- sacred altar cloth
- crystals or a crystal grid: choose a crystal medicine that reflects the intention for your altar
- photo or figurine of your chosen angel, goddess, god or deity
- photo or item that represents your ancestors
- something to represent the earth, such as sage or flowers
- something to represent fire, such as a candle
- something to represent water, such as a bowl of water or a vase
- something to represent air, such as a feather
- one item each to represent the four directions
- something special and sacred to represent you and your journey
- personal affirmations
- any other items that represent the intention of your altar.

To activate, energise and bless your altar:

- Take a moment to connect into the light of the universe.
- Light and burn some sage to cleanse the space.
- Light a candle.
- Call in all your spirit beings and helpers that walk with you in spirit.
- Call in your ancestors.
- Call in all the devas of the items on your altar.
- Ask that all these beings assist you in your intention.
- State your intention for your altar out loud.
- Activate your crystal grid if you have one.

Make sure to tend to your altar each day to recharge it and keep it activated. Refresh any water daily and burn sage to keep the space cleansed.

ADVANCED HEALING PRACTICES

CHAPTER 27

THIRTEEN STEPS OF ADVANCED HEALING FOR PRACTITIONERS

It's important to have a solid understanding and foundation before facilitating healing on other people. In this section of the book I provide details on how to create a safe and sacred space for facilitating healing on others, from connecting with your client through to self-care after the healing and everything in between. Please make sure you familiarise yourself with the 13 steps before facilitating the advanced healings.

These are the steps to work through during a crystal healing session:

1. Prepare the healing space.
2. Prepare yourself.
3. Attune yourself with your client.

4. Hydrate your client and yourself.

5. Select and cleanse your crystals and healing tools.

6. Place the crystals on your client's body.

7. Invoke guidance.

8. Relax your client and get them to focus on their breathing.

9. Facilitate your chosen healing process.

10. Finish the healing.

11. Decide on an ongoing integration and nurturing plan.

12. Fill in the healing record form.

13. Cleanse your crystals and separate yourself from the healing.

STEP 1: PREPARE THE HEALING SPACE

It's important to prepare and cleanse your healing space prior to any healing. When working with energy healing your client will become sensitive and vulnerable to the energy that is present in the space, so as a healer it is your responsibility to make sure the space is clean on every level; it is a part of your occupational health and safety responsibilities. If the space is not cleansed your client can pick up unwanted energies.

There are several ways to cleanse a healing space, the first being to set a strong intention that you would like your space clear and to be of the highest vibrational energy possible. The most popular way to create a clean and sacred space is by using sacred herbs such as sage or eucalyptus leaves, herbs that have been used for thousands of years to honour and cleanse people, places and things. Another great tool for energetically clearing a room and lifting its vibration is through using sound with items such as Tibetan bells, crystal bowls, medicine drums, rattles, healing music and even your own voice. It's also a great idea to call in your spirit healers from the other side to assist in cleansing and bringing in high-vibration energy. I like to call on Archangel Michael and ask that he puts a protective shield around the space to keep us safe from lower energies.

Before every healing it's encouraged and important to honour the land on which you stand, sending love to all the spirits that reside in this sacred

space and honouring and paying your respects to the original Traditional Custodians and the caretakers of the land past, present and future. I also like to set an objective that I come to this land with an intention of love, peace and healing.

Other ways to set the space is by lighting a candle, creating crystal grids and making sure the space is tidy and inviting. Before and after each healing make sure that you cleanse and recharge the space.

STEP 2: PREPARE YOURSELF

It's important to get yourself energetically ready and prepared for each healing. Take a few minutes to attune to your higher self, your crystals and any medicine or tools you will be using, opening your heart in love and gratitude. Before you work on others make sure you have a deep understating of and your own relationship with the tools and medicine you're using. Using your breath and intention, calm your mind as you connect with a place of peace within.

Giving and receiving crystal healings are both acts of meditation, so it is very important to stay in the present moment. You will be better able to attune to the needs of your client if you are centred and conscious in the now. Make sure to continue your healing journey in your own life so you can hold a deep and powerful space for your client.

STEP 3: ATTUNE YOURSELF WITH YOUR CLIENT

Offering healing to others is a very vulnerable and intimate experience. It's vital to create a safe and sacred emotional space for your client. Always approach your client with a loving open energy and help to make them feel as welcome and safe as you can. When people find their way into your healing space it's usually at the stage where they are really wanting help and just want someone to hear, support and understand them. It's important to sit in sacred space with your client and listen with an open heart and empathy. Healing can only occur when your client feels safe with you, which will create a connection; trust is a huge part of the healing.

Filling out a client record form for a new client is a great way to start building a connection and trust with your client. Make sure you fill out the form together. The questions on the form will help you decide what healing would be the best for your client and their intentions and helps you choose the crystals and medicine you will work with. A great reference tool for understanding what is causing energy blockages is Annette Noontil's book *The Body is the Barometer of the Soul*.

NAME:

ADDRESS:

PHONE:

EMAIL:

DATE OF BIRTH:

ARE YOU SEEING ANOTHER THERAPIST? IF SO, GIVE DETAILS:

HAVE YOU EVER HAD ANY EXPERIENCES WITH CRYSTALS OR HEALING? IF SO, GIVE DETAILS:

WHAT IS YOUR INTENTION FOR THIS SESSION?

ARE THERE ANY HEALTH CONCERNS AFFECTING YOU?

PHYSICALLY:

MENTALLY:

EMOTIONALLY:

SPIRITUALLY:

STEP 4: HYDRATE YOUR CLIENT AND YOURSELF

Make sure that you and your client are well hydrated before and after healing. Water is a strong conduit of energy and assists in the movement of energy through and around the body. If someone is dehydrated the energy can get stuck and not flow to where it is needed. Crystals as well as people are also made up of a large percentage of water; therefore the interaction between the water element in the body and in the crystals plays an important role in the healing. Toxins can be released into the body during a healing, and the best way to clear them is by drinking lots of water to flush them from your system.

STEP 5: SELECT AND CLEANSE YOUR CRYSTALS AND HEALING TOOLS

It's extremely important to always work with cleansed and charged crystals because, as you know, they hold and store energy from those who have handled them before you. Once you start working with a range of crystals and understanding their energy it will be easier for you to choose which crystals will be best for the healing. Have your client choose up to 10 crystals: they may be crystals your client has brought with them or be from your own collection. Inviting your client to be a part of their own healing process is very empowering; their soul knows exactly what medicine they require and the law of attraction will energetically guide them to what crystals they need to assist them in their healing.

Take notice of what crystals they choose, as this will indicate where their healing may take them. You can guide them in choosing the crystals by suggesting they close their eyes and set an intention to be guided to the perfect crystals for them for the healing. When they open their eyes they will be directly guided to the perfect crystals for them. They may just feel a strong pull to a crystal, they may see it shining more than others or be excited and attracted by its shape or colour. Remind them that they can never choose the wrong crystal and encourage them in the process.

You will also intuitively choose as many crystals as you feel appropriate. Trust your guidance on this and make sure to use the suggested crystals I offer under each process in this book.

STEP 6: PLACE THE CRYSTALS ON YOUR CLIENT'S BODY

Place the crystal/s intuitively on your client's body and on the chakras where guided. Make sure you trust yourself with this, as crystals have an innate intelligence of their own and the crystal energy will go directly to where it is needed. Be guided by your intuition and the energy of the crystal.

Some crystals may fall off during the healing, but there is no need to place them back on your client's body as they have offered their energy and have chosen to leave the body. Be open to the guidance from other crystals that may want to join in on the healing as you go. You may get a sense of a crystal calling your attention, so make sure you listen to this and bring it into your healing.

STEP 7: INVOKE GUIDANCE

When we offer healing we tune in to the unconditional love of the cosmos and become a pure conduit of universal healing energy. We also have a team in the spirit world ready and waiting to assist us in this healing space. It's important to honour these beings and call upon their love, support and guidance. When you are new to healing you may not know who your guides are and that is fine, as you will get to know them in time and the more you do healing. If you're unsure of your guides it's still important to call upon them anyway and trust that they are with you in the healing; sometimes you may feel them while at other times you may not.

The more you work with your guides the easier it will be to sense them. You can call upon Archangel Raphael, the angel of healing, to be with you if you're not confident or sure about your guides. Raphael supports all the healers of the world, and all you need to do is call upon his assistance and he will be with you.

It's important also to honour all the medicine you are working with in the healing. Take time to call upon the spirit of this energy. For example,

it's a great idea to call in your power animals, the devas of the crystals you're working with, Mother Earth, universal love, great spirit and any other medicine you are connecting with in the healing. It's a good idea to also call in the guides, spirit helpers, animal totems, ancestors and higher self of your client.

Before each healing you will set and hold the intention that this healing is for your client's highest good. This will allow the healing to be guided by the highest form of love possible and move beyond the ego's intentions, opening your client to receive healing from a higher perspective. You will also ask that your client's intentions are answered; however, sometimes there is a higher purpose and this statement allows for that energy to guide the healing.

Before you start the healing, a powerful way to create a sacred and safe space is to call in your spirit team and say an invocation that helps to create a safe, loving environment. Below is a calling and invocation for reference, although I invite you at some point to create your own that resonate with you.

Calling upon guides and spirit helpers

For this step you say:

> *I call on universal love and light to work through me as I become a pure channel of love. I call in Archangel Raphael, the angel of healing, and ask to be a conduit of divine healing light. I ask that my heart becomes a healing heart and my hands become channels of divine healing energy. I call upon my spirit team, crystal devas, angels, guides, ancestors, animal totems, allies and any beings from the light and any earth medicine that would like to assist in the healing to come in and help to create this sacred healing space.*
> *I call upon Archangel Michael to place us in a protective shield of light where only spirits of the light all enter. I ask that you are our protector in the spirit world and to keep us safe.*

I call [your client's name]*'s spirit team, angels, guides, ancestors, animal totems and any beings from the light and any earth medicine that would like to assist in the healing to come in and help create this sacred healing space. I call on* [your client's name]*'s highest self to come forth and be present in this healing and relay to their heart, mind, body and spirit whatever is needed at this time to gain understanding and healing.*

Invocation

Say the following invocation three times:

I invoke the love of the divine universe within my heart.
I am a clear and pure channel.
Love is my guide.

Then say once:

I follow this love.

STEP 8: RELAX YOUR CLIENT AND GET THEM TO FOCUS ON THEIR BREATHING

Breathing is extremely important in healing: we can go without many things in life but we can live without breathing for only a very short time. The breath is truly sacred and brings life; the more breath you can draw into your body the more universal light will enter each cell.

Breathing is our main source of life energy, as on the inhalation we receive energy and on the exhalation we give it back. Over time we have forgotten how to breathe properly, with most of us taking shallow breaths

from the lungs that are known as fight or flight breaths. This breathing is created due to living in a fast-paced world and having a busy lifestyle; our senses are overloaded and our bodies feel the need to fight or flight. Our breathing follows suit.

To breathe correctly is to take big, deep, long belly breaths in which our bodies and lungs become full of air. When we breathe in this manner it naturally calms the nervous system, relaxes the mind and balances emotions.

Becoming aware of your breathing is one of the most powerful ways of staying in the present moment. Encourage your client to breathe long and deep to assist in bringing in the light of the universe, which will naturally help to heal the mind, body and spirit. When a blockage or emotions come to the surface your client can start to hold their breath, and when breathing is held in it shuts down the energy flow in the body and energy can get stuck and stagnate. Encouraging your client to breathe allows for the energy to flow and assists in the release of stale emotions and thoughts. Maintain focus on your client's breathing throughout the healing, as this will give you an indication of where they are emotionally and enable you to assist them in breathing through blockages when they come up. When this happens you could gently say something like the following in a soft calm voice:

I invite you to take a big deep breath in, and on the exhale let go of any concerns, worries, stress or emotions. Take another big inhale and drop deeper within, then exhale and let go, let it all go, relax and completely surrender.

STEP 9: FACILITATE YOUR CHOSEN HEALING PROCESS

To do this, choose any healing process in this book.

STEP 10: FINISH THE HEALING

You will know when the healing is complete as you will feel the energy disperse and the energy in the room may feel different. As all healings are unique the timeframe on a healing can differ; however, I have found that they commonly take around one to one and a half hours. They will naturally come to an end, usually after a big realisation, release and shift. Make sure to be open and connected with your client's process so you know the right cues to take.

It is always nice to give your client a beautiful sound bath, working with any type of sound instrument such as a crystal bowl, Tibetan bowl, chimes, bells, tuning forks, rain stick or drum. Give your client's feet a little rub, as this will help to ground them. Offering them a cup of tea or some water is another good idea. I also like to share a prayer over my client while they are still lying on the table, usually positive words going forward that are directly connected to what came up in the healing.

When the healing has finished, take the crystals off your client's body while you ask them to focus on their breathing. Bring them back into their body by saying something such as:

> *Come back into the room, back into your body, into the here and now, and slowly open your eyes, feeling completely grounded and revitalised.*

Once the healing is complete, make sure to thank all the guides, crystal devas and spirits of the medicine you connected with. Remember that you don't have to do everything in one healing session, as it is a process. Your client will require time to integrate the healing and incorporate the effects of it in their day-to-day life using the maintenance plan you suggest to them.

STEP 11: DECIDE ON AN ONGOING INTEGRATION AND NURTURING PLAN

The healing is only the beginning of the process, and your client will require time to integrate the energy. They may feel many different sensations and feelings after a healing depending on what came up in the session: some may feel on top of the world while others may feel drained and tired and anything in between. These types of energetic healings can go very deep and emotions can come to the surface, and it takes time to process this old energy.

It's a good idea to share with your client that they may feel emotional or a little off but that this is normal and it will pass as the energy integrates. They will feel lighter and clearer after a few days as their energy comes back into balance. It's important to share with your client the different possibilities that could happen once they leave the healing space so they know that how they are feeling is perfectly normal.

To support this process and your client after the healing it is beneficial to set an ongoing nurturing plan for them to ensure the healing that has occurred can be fully embodied and integrated. By suggesting an ongoing healing plan you are also empowering your client to take responsibility for their own healing and to not become dependent on you as the healer. The role of a crystal healer is to be there and assist in your client's own healing process, as true empowerment comes when they personally claim their inner light and learn how to be one with themselves in daily life. You will know intuitively which plan will be most effective for your client by the nature of the healing and what came up for them.

Below are some suggestions to include in an integration and nurturing plan.

Meditation

The process of meditation allows us to let go of our worries, defrag and cleanse our minds. It is a time of relaxation and renewal for the mind, body and soul, and during it we receive inner guidance, insight, clarity and spiritual growth. Meditation in the morning can set your attitude for the day, while meditation last thing at night allows your mind to relax and let go of the day.

Suggest to your client they meditate for at least 15 minutes every day to assist in their personal growth. There are many ways of meditating;

it does not have to be sitting cross-legged on the floor with your eyes shut. For some people meditating could be walking on the beach, riding a bike or sitting quietly in a park. As long as you are taking time out for yourself to just be then it's a form of meditation.

Affirmations

Affirmations are a powerful way of reprogramming old thought patterns to new ones to create transformation and positive change in your life. Thoughts are what shape and create your reality, and affirming the change you want in your life is a very effective way of manifesting a fresh reality. If your client is using negative self-talk or you have pinpointed a belief system and thought pattern in the healing that is holding them back, give them a positive affirmation that relates to the healing. For example, if something came up in the healing that indicated they don't trust themselves, you could suggest an affirmation such as *'I completely trust in myself in all situations in every moment.'* You might even want to get them to suggest their own affirmation, which can be more effective because they have chosen it and it resonates most fully with them.

You can also explain to your client how to program a crystal so they can use this method to amplify their affirmation.

Yoga, walking or any type of exercise

Exercising is a powerful way to release and move energy, allowing the body to heal itself. It also clears and balances the chakra system. Yoga balances the body, mind, emotions and spirit and calms the mind, and in this space we gain a sense of perspective that brings feelings of peace, freedom and inner strength. A simple act of walking can encourage energy to move around the body, and the release of endorphins allows for feelings of well-being.

Suggest to your client to undertake some form of exercise and make sure it's something your client enjoys. They will benefit on a range of levels and gain better overall health.

Individual work with crystals

Working closely and individually with crystals can assist greatly in the ongoing healing of your client. It is best to suggest a crystal that will

directly help bring healing to the issues or imbalances that came up in the healing. Suggest your client carry the crystal around with them, sleep with it and work with it in meditation. You may have the crystal for your client to buy or guide them to a place that does. You may also like to offer them a crystal essence if you have one on hand.

Nurturing

After the healing the energies will continue to integrate, a process that can last for a few days. Emotions may continue to come up for your client in the days after the healing, so it is important for them to be gentle with themselves.

The physical and emotional bodies need time out to rest and recuperate. Below are some suggestions for nurturing the mind, body and soul that you might like to suggest to your client:

- Soak in an Epsom salt bath, adding essential oils to relax their mind and body such as lavender, chamomile, geranium and sandalwood.
- Take a walk in nature.
- Take some time out, some play time, to do what they love to do.
- Walk along the beach then swim in the ocean.
- Write, draw, paint, hang out with friends or just hang out with themselves.

STEP 12: FILL IN THE HEALING RECORD FORM

Record the main aspects of the healing on the client record form, and if required set a date for your client to come back for another session. This information is very beneficial when a client returns for a healing as you can go back over your notes and familiarise yourself with what happened in the previous session, which will help you to create a deeper bond with your client and assist you to go deep into the current healing.

Due to your client's privacy, make sure these forms are kept in a locked cabinet.

Crystal shamanism healing record

NAME: _____

DATE: _____

RECORD THE CRYSTALS THAT WERE USED: _____

_____

_____

_____

RECORD THE NATURE OF THE HEALING: _____

_____

_____

_____

_____

_____

_____

FURTHER HEALING TO BE DONE, INCLUDING THE NEXT HEALING DATE:

_____

_____

_____

_____

NURTURING PLAN SUGGESTION: _____

_____

_____

_____

STEP 13: CLEANSE YOUR CRYSTALS AND SEPARATE YOURSELF FROM THE HEALING

After each healing it is very important to cleanse all your crystals and take a few moments in meditation to separate yourself from the healing, severing any etheric cords and cleansing yourself with golden light. At times in the healing space you can take on unwanted energies and emotions and the healing can also trigger and bring up your own, so it's super important to cleanse yourself. If this is not done it can easily drain you and leave you feeling burned out and exhausted.

Make sure you do personal ongoing healing and look after yourself so you can hold a loving, powerful and sacred space for your clients.

CHAPTER 28

SHAMANIC HEALING TOOLS AND MEDICINE USED IN ADVANCED HEALING PRACTICES

In the next couple of advanced healing processes you will be utilising a range of different shamanic tools and medicine. Overall, this medicine will assist in a deep cleansing of your client's mind, body and spirit and will set a pure and sacred space for them to go deep so they can receive a lot more from the healing. The following is an explanation of what this medicine offers in the healing space.

Sage: sage is a sacred plant used by shamans in ceremony and rituals for clearing energy and setting sacred space, and it is brought into a healing

to do exactly that: cleanse any unwanted or lower energies from the aura and also to honour the client. You set the intention that the smoke from the sage will send all the intentions and prayers to great spirit or the great creator. You will also set the intention that the sage will be an offering to all the medicines you will work with in the healing to create your own connection and relationship with the medicine before you work with it.

Drums: when you play a drum be guided by your intuition and call upon its spirit to allow the drum to play through you. Drums are utilised in healings for two different purposes.

First, their sounds and vibrations shake up any suppressed energy in the body and bring it to the surface to be released. There is no specific drumbeat; it's more about setting the intention to heal, balance and release energy from your client's field that's not serving them on all levels of their being. Drum sounds and vibrations have an innate intelligence of their own and the medicine will naturally invite the cells of the body to return to their natural healthy state of being.

The second aspect of working with drums is setting the intention to invoke and offer the actual medicine of the drum. Each drum has its own energy depending on its skin and spirit. For example, the medicine of kangaroo skin is all about moving forward and clearing a path and the medicine of deer skin is all about healing the heart and gentleness and kindness. Work with the specific medicine so your client can feel the energy resonate into every cell of their being. The more you play the drum the deeper your relationship with it will be, making it a lot easier to work with and understand its purpose and medicine in your healings.

Feathers: you may work with any feather you feel drawn to, as it's important that you obtain a connection with the medicine of the feather before you start. As you bring in the feather you will set the intention to be a conduit for its energy; you will become the bird and offer this medicine to your client. The feather will help you to clear any energy that was brought up by the drum, and working hand in hand with the element of air will help to clear this energy from your client's aura and energy field.

Hands on: there is something very comforting about having hands placed upon you in a loving and healing way. When you place your hands on your client you are offering support and comfort as well as channelling

healing energy to them. It will also assist in relaxing your client as they are invited to drop even deeper into the stillness and sacred healing space. Close your eyes, open to being a pure channel and conduit and allow your spirit helpers and guides to channel the loving, healing energy of the universe through you to your client. This process is very intuitive, so make sure you listen to your own guidance and place your hands where you feel guided to.

Activating crystal energy: this part of the healing will create an opportunity for your client to connect deeply with crystal medicine and understand the breathing and sounds that amplify this connection. Encourage your client to take long, deep breaths, which will turn on crystal energy as well as open your client to receiving more energy.

Sound is also an amplifier of energy, so you can play a crystal bowl or Tibetan bell while your client breathes deeply. Sound has an innate healing intelligence and will permeate into the cells of your client. Working with sound with intent creates a sacred healing space in which your client will naturally open and receive on a deep level. Sound healing expands beyond the logical thinking mind and bathes the mind, body and spirit with pure vibration.

In the activating crystal energy part of the practice you will guide your client to connect deeply with the earth and universal light energy. The three main healing energies utilised in these powerful healings are the crystals or earth medicines, the medicine of Mother Earth herself and the great spirit of universal energy. These energies have a huge part to play in the potency of the healing.

CHAPTER 29

CRYSTAL AWAKENING SHAMANISM HEALING

In a crystal awakening healing you will guide your client into an awakening crystal, where they will meet the deva and receive healing. You will then guide them into a cave to meet someone in the spirit world, where they will receive a sacred gift and message.

THE MEDICINE OF CRYSTAL AWAKENING

The main medicine of this healing is connecting with and receiving the energy of the awakening crystal, commonly known as elestial quartz, and meeting a special person in the spirit world to receive healing, wisdom and a sacred gift. The awakening crystal is a potent medicine that will assist

to heal the emotional body and is also a gift from the angels to humanity for overall healing on a global scale.

This practice outlined is a guide only, and once you get familiar with the essence and intention of the healing you are encouraged to use your own wording. The ultimate goal is to hold space and channel your guidance and healing within the intention of the process. I strongly encourage you do this healing on yourself first so you are familiar with the process and crystal energy. Crystal awakening shamanism healing will benefit anyone who needs:

- general healing or direction
- guidance from a spirit helper
- emotional healing
- a connection with someone who has passed
- past-life healing.

MY PERSONAL EXPERIENCE

In Chapter 4 I related my personal story of the eagle medicine, about spending time in Sedona with a shaman. He took me through a very powerful healing journey in which I met my father in another life as a chief of the tribe. The healing was so powerful and tangible I now offer this healing to others in my practice. I have changed the healing over the years; however, the essence is the same. Please make sure to read the eagle story before facilitating an awakening healing, as it's important to understand where it originated from.

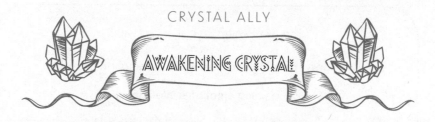

CRYSTAL ALLY

AWAKENING CRYSTAL

The awakening crystal, or elestial quartz, is one of the most powerful crystals on earth and a true gift to our planet at its time of transformation. It holds within it the secrets to healing the emotional body on a large scale, working with group consciousness and assisting the planet in bringing oneness to our world community. They are a gift from the angels to help us through a deep emotional healing on a mass scale. Connecting with an awakening crystal allows you to receive clarity in relation to your emotional wounds, gaining a sense of emotional intelligence and well-being. It amplifies buried emotions, allowing them to surface while supporting and holding you as you delve deep into the wound. As your heart opens and self-love is experienced your awareness expands to receive the gift from such a challenge. Once these emotions are brought into balance you will feel less addiction, depression, anxiety and separation in your life and feel more connected, having a sense of freedom and an inner peace. Awakening crystals are great for anyone who has embarked on a journey of loving and accepting the shadow side of their psyche because it holds a safe, powerful space to look deep within your hidden chambers. It also assists in creating awareness around why and how people trigger you. If someone pushes your emotional buttons they give you an opportunity to see this trait in yourself, a trait that has been unloved or forgotten. Awakening crystals hold sacred space for a deep opening of your mind and heart and dissolve the emotional trigger, allowing you to see the truth of how the emotion was first created. In this process you are able to stop projecting onto others and take back your personal power and responsibility, setting you free from your emotional chains.

The awakening crystal assists with:

※ deep clearing and healing on an emotional level

※ gaining emotional intelligence

※ releasing and transforming grief, fear and trauma

※ dissolving old wounds of the past

※ understanding the depth of the self

※ accepting the dying process

※ understanding your shadow self

※ overcoming addiction

※ healing your nervous system.

PRACTITIONER HEALING

The words that are provided below to share with your client throughout their journey are a guide only. The more you do the healings the more you will understand the intention, outcome and the energy of the healing and eventually you will use your own words as support. When you guide your client through the process make sure to take it slowly, pause between words and allow time for your client to have an experience. Don't just read the script: you need to hold sacred healing space as you share the words and guide your client and be aware of what's happening for them. Use a soft voice and stop if your client gets emotional or overwhelmed. Stop, allow for the healing energy to integrate, and when it feels right start up again where you finished off.

Follow this process when you undertake a healing for your client:

※ Prepare the healing space by cleansing it.

※ Prepare and centre yourself.

※ Attune yourself with your client by filling in the client record form (see Chapter 27).

- Make sure you and your client are well hydrated.
- Ask your client to choose 10 crystals, which you will lay on their chakra points and any other parts of their body you are intuitively guided to. Make sure one of them is an awakening crystal.
- Set and state out loud your client's intention and add that this healing is for the highest good of all and from the highest place of love possible.
- Invoke guidance from the angels, guides, crystal devas, animal guides and any other beings that would like to assist in the healing by saying this invocation out loud:

I invoke the love of the divine universe within my heart
I am a clear and pure channel
Love is my guide.

I invoke the love of the divine universe within my heart
I am a clear and pure channel
Love is my guide.

I invoke the love of the divine universe within my heart
I am a clear and pure channel
Love is my guide.

And I follow that love.

- Bring yourself into your heart centre by connecting with universal love and Mother Earth. Visualise this energy moving through your crown chakra to your heart and down your arms and into your hands. Allow yourself to be a channel of divine love and healing.
- Light sage and direct the smoke over your client with a feather. You say:

I ask that the sacred smoke from this sage sends all our prayers
and intentions for this healing to our divine creator. I offer you

this sacred sage as an honouring of your mind, body and spirit for every breath you have ever taken and for every step you have walked upon this earth. You are blessed.

- Work with the medicine of your drum. Spend five minutes drumming around and over your client, sending love and healing energy. Do this without speaking.
- Work with a feather and set the intention of clearing old energy from the aura as you guide the feather over your client's body to remove and dissolve the old energy.
- Place your hands on your client's feet for a few minutes, then their knees, abdomen, heart, the sides of their face and the top of their head. This will allow your client to relax and drop deep into a sacred space of receiving. Do this in silence for five to 10 minutes, and make sure to channel the healing energy of the universe as you open to be a pure channel.
- Guide your client to connect deeply with the universe, earth and crystals. You say:

Visualise a beautiful golden light streaming down from the heavens and into the top of your head. Feel this healing light move into your heart and allow your heart to pulsate this light through your whole body and into every single cell of your being.

Guide your client using your own words to connect deeply with the golden healing light of the universe and send it through their body and into every cell of their being.

- Guide your client to connect with Mother Earth. You say:

Visualise a root extending down from the bottom of your spine. Send this root deep into the earth, down, down, deep down into

the centre of the earth. Anchor your roots into the heart of Mother Gaia. She becomes aware of your presence, and she sends you her loving, nurturing, nourishing, healing energy. Breathe this up into your spine and into your heart. Allow your heart to send this healing energy into the rest of your body.

Guide your client using your own words to receive the love and blessings of the earth.

⟪ Guide your client to connect deeply with the crystals by encouraging them to take very long, deep breaths for five minutes. As they breathe and connect, play a crystal bowl to amplify energy and say the following:

Bring your awareness to your heart. On your in breath, breathe the energy of the universe and the earth into your heart. On your out breath, send this energy out to the crystals. On your next in breath, breathe the energy of the crystals into your heart. On your out breath, send this crystal healing energy into every cell of your being.

⟪ Use your own words and listen to your intuition to facilitate your client's deep connection with the crystals and sending this energy into their body. Make sure you encourage them to take long, deep breaths to amplify the healing energy.

You will now guide your client to journey inside the awakening crystal to meet a spirit helper and receive healing from the crystal.

⟪ You say:

It is time to journey inside the crystal. Send a beam of pink light and unconditional love from your heart deeply into the heart

of the crystal. Draw your awareness down through the light as you enter into the centre of the crystal, allowing yourself to drop deeply into the heart of the crystal. You have now arrived deep within the inner chamber of the awakening crystal and to meet you there is the crystal's deva. Take a moment to introduce yourself and connect. The deva would like to offer you some healing and sends this powerful healing energy into your heart. Open and receive this deeply.

- Play a medicine drum softly into your client's heart to amplify the healing energy and use your own words and guidance to facilitate a deep opening and healing. You say:

Now the deva would like to take you to a very sacred cave where there is someone special awaiting your arrival; it could be an ancestor, guide, ascended master, animal or spirit helper. Journey to this cave now, and when you arrive take a moment to connect deeply with this sacred place. The special person walks over to you now, so take a moment to feel, see and connect with them. Take your time. This special soul has arrived to offer you a gift that will assist in your healing. Receive this gift now: place it in your heart and feel its powerful healing energy pulsating through the whole of your mind, body and spirit. This special being now has a very important message for you to assist in your continuous healing; receive this message now. Know that you are loved and supported in the spirit world at all times and they have heard your prayers and intentions.

- Use your own guidance and intuition to facilitate the connection from this special being in spirit. You say:

It is time to return; take a moment to thank the deva and your special guide for the healing. Start drawing your awareness out from the crystal into the physical plane as you bring all aspects of self back into the here and now.

⋘ Finish the healing by placing your hands on your client's head and sending love into their being. Next, place your hands on your client's feet and set the intention to bring your client back into their body and into the now.

⋘ Use a drum or bells to close the healing as you direct this sound over your client's body.

⋘ Gently bring your client back into the room and fully back into their body. Bring their conscious awareness to the present moment: right here, right now.

⋘ Ask your client to thank their guides, angels, crystal devas, animal spirits and any other beings that assisted in the healing.

⋘ Fill in the client record form (see Chapter 27).

⋘ Cleanse your crystals and separate yourself from the healing.

CHAPTER 30

CUTTING ENERGETIC CORDS

Energetic or etheric cords are created when you have a co-dependent relationship with another person, object, place or thing. They are cords of energy that attach from an unhealthy bond to something. These cords can drain you of energy and make you feel stuck and stagnant and can cause feelings of guilt and obligation. They are nothing to be ashamed of or worried about, as they are a natural part of having a human connection and in most cases can be easily severed.

THE MEDICINE OF CUTTING ENERGETIC CORDS

Just as you need to wash your physical body when it is dirty, cutting etheric cords is a way of cleansing your energy and emotional body. You can have energetic cords with your children, parents, friends, partners, work

colleagues and clients and you can even have cords with material things such as houses, places and inanimate objects. Problems can arise when you have too many cords and they start to affect your life.

Energetic cords can also be created when two people have karmic ties or a contract together. When a soul contract between two people isn't finished, a strong energetic tie binds them and keeps pulling them back together like a magnet. This is especially so with romantic connections, as sometimes the vows from past lifetimes can spill over to the current life. The karmic contract pulls them back together and the couple find it difficult to leave the relationship. These cords can also be created in relationships where one person is controlling over the other. In this case the cords can become very strong, and a toxic pattern of unhealthy co- dependence and attachment is created.

During your lifetime you will constantly be creating cords with other people due to your emotional connection and the bonds you have in your relationships; the deeper the emotional connection the bigger the cord. You are an energetic being who is sensitive to other people's energy and emotions, and when you have a negative experience with another person or feel worried or concerned for them an energetic cord is created. This cord can make you feel tired and depressed and you can feel out of sorts for no specific reason. The good news is that once understood these cords can be easily severed by working with a simple process that includes intention and love.

Cords can also be formed when there is an unhealthy attachment to things or places; for example, you may be attached to a home you need to sell but you're finding it difficult because you have many precious memories of living there and are sad to leave this place you called home for so long. The emotional bond you have with the home can prevent the house from selling, so you need to cut the cords and set yourself emotionally free from it. Another example is when you are addicted to something and over time you build a toxic bond and create etheric cords to the addiction. There are many layers to an addiction; however, cutting the cords can be a helpful process to assist you in the start of letting go of this unhealthy bond and negative influence in your life.

When you cut the energetic cords with those you love it's important to remember you can never sever the bonds of love between two people,

just the dysfunctional cords that keep you bound in a negative pattern or relationship. When cutting cords it's an important part of the process to practise unconditional love, as this will help sever the cords and deepen the connection of a healthy relationship. Parents can sometimes feel a little unsure about cutting cords to their children as they feel it's their responsibility to look after their children and that cutting cords is cutting themselves out of the child's life. However, when cutting etheric cords you are cutting the unhealthy emotional cords and strengthening the bonds of love.

Once unhealthy cords have been severed between two people or between a person and an object they can feel a deeper connection of love and a sense of emotional freedom. It helps them come back into their own energy field and feel refreshed, balanced and renewed. When the energetic cords from toxic relationships have been severed it will make room for fresh, healthier connections. Cutting energetic cords will benefit anyone who:

- has unhealthy attachments to a person, place or thing
- finds it hard to leave an unhealthy relationship
- worries constantly about other people
- struggles in a co-dependent relationship
- has conflict or experiences challenges with someone.

MY PERSONAL EXPERIENCE

I first came across the concept of etheric cords when I was working with Doreen Virtue in her angel intuitive workshops. I was fascinated by the process, and after years of seeing so many people benefit from it I started to use it in my own life and practice. My understanding of cord cutting and karmic ties has grown extensively over the years, and my cord-cutting process has changed and developed into a very powerful one that addresses many layers. There are so many levels you can explore when cord cutting, from a simple intention of cutting cords to the intricate process of working with the lords of karma, which is the process I share below.

CRYSTAL ALLY

ANCIENT
HEALING CRYSTAL

Ancient healing crystals, commonly known as laser wands, hold within them the secrets of crystal healing and have been used by many healers and shamans throughout history. When you are blessed with the opportunity to connect with one of these amazing tools you will awaken to the knowledge of the sacred laws of healing held within its energy. Each crystal has its own unique energy and when aligned to its sacred deva it will share with you its secrets and how to work with it. For those who know how, these sacred crystals are used as psychic surgery tools and a powerful tool for cutting etheric cords. These crystals assists with:

- cutting emotional cords to people

- creating protective shields

- performing psychic surgery

- connecting with ancient wisdom and the laws of healing.

PRACTITIONER HEALING

In this process you will work with an ancient healing crystal, Archangel Michael and the lords of karma, all very important parts of the process that bring their specific medicine to the healing. The ancient healing crystal deva will help to cut the cords on a physical and energetic level; Archangel Michael works with his sword of light to cut emotional cords; and the lords of karma work on a soul level severing karmic ties.

The lords of karma are a group of evolved beings who work with souls before they incarnate to work out their karma. Generally speaking,

as a healer you don't have the power to sever or dissolve karmic contract. You can, however, invite your client to give permission for the lords of karma to intervene. You explain this to your client then invite them, if they are ready to open their heart, to give permission to the lords, who will work with your client on a soul level.

In relationships we hand over to each other parts of ourselves such as our power, trust and different aspects of our soul. We can also place fears, beliefs, expectations, opinions, obligations and many other things upon each other, which can put a lot of strain on the connection and leave us feeling trapped and unhappy in the relationship. One of the most powerful and important parts of the cord-cutting process is giving your client the opportunity to retrieve these parts of themselves and hand back anything that's not of their soul's essence. This is a powerful way to set both parties free from old, stale energy and restraints.

Throughout the healing practice, invite an honest discussion between your client and get them to call in the higher self of the person with whom they are cutting the cords. This is the aspect of a person's soul that is all loving, all wise and all knowing; it is the part of the soul that doesn't judge and understands and sees things from a place of unconditional love. Invite your client to share with the higher self of the other person anything that is weighing on them, such as things they can't say to the other person's face.

Sometimes due to rejection and fear of conflict we refrain from sharing our deeper truths, but in this process your client is encouraged to be completely honest and invited to share everything they are feeling, to get everything off their chest while knowing this is a safe space to let go of any burdens and worries they may be feeling. Get your client to visualise the other person's higher self in a golden sphere of light. The person is not there physically in the healing, but your client can call in this higher-self aspect of the soul to energetically enter the sacred healing space.

This process can be extremely therapeutic and creates a safe and receptive space to communicate without rejection, reaction and denial from the person they are severing the cords with. Follow this procedure to perform a cord-cutting healing for your client:

⋙ Discuss with them who they would like to cut cords with. You say:

We invoke and call upon the higher self of [the name of the person your client is cutting cords with] *and ask the all-loving, all-knowing and wise aspect of self to join us in this sacred healing space.*

❧ Ask your client to visualise this person in a golden sphere of light and give them a moment to arrive and connect. You say:

Is there anything you would like to say or share with this person? Express everything that has been concerning you; this is your time to get everything off your chest. Positive and negative, make sure to be true and real and honest with yourself and the other person about how you feel.

❧ Hold a nurturing energetic space while your client communicates. You say:

It is time to allow [the name of the person your client wants to cut cords with] *to share. Tune into and feel what they have to say, making sure not to take anything negative on but just allowing a space of listening.*

❧ Hold a nurturing energetic space while your client listens. You say:

This is the perfect opportunity to energetically retrieve any aspect of yourself you have handed over or that this person may have taken from you over time. Feel into your relationship with this person and become aware of anything that this connection has taken from you, things such as your power, trust or light. Ask for these parts of yourself back and make sure to be present and aware of each aspect

as you see the other person hand them back to you and you return them to your heart.

❧ Hold a nurturing energetic space while your client retrieves these aspects. You say:

It is time to give back any aspect you may have taken or this person may have handed over to you. Tune in to your body and feel if you are holding anything of the other person's energy. Gather it up as an energy ball and hand it back to them.

❧ This is a very powerful process, so allow your client some time to experience this before saying:

Now that you have retrieved all of the parts of yourself it is time to cut any old energetic cords and dissolve any old karmic ties between you. We call upon the lords of karma and ask them to join us in this sacred healing space. We also call upon Archangel Michael to bring his powerful sword of light and upon the deva of the ancient healing crystal.

It is time to give permission as you tune in to your heart and set an intention that you are willing to dissolve and sever any contracts or agreements that you may have with [person's name]. *It is time to let each other go and set yourself free.*

We ask the lords of karma to intervene and sever and dissolve any old contracts, promises, vows and attachments between these two people that are not serving them any longer and ask that this is for their highest good.

❧ Hold space while the lords of karma facilitate healing on a soul level. You could play a crystal bowl if you like or simply act as a channel of light for the lords of karma. Once you feel like the clearing has been completed you say:

Allow yourself to feel or see any energetic cords that may still be binding you both. Become aware of these cords. Take a deep breath in as we ask Archangel Michael to cut through any cords with his sword of love and light. On your out breath, see these cords dissolve or sever.

You may have to do this process a few times, feeling into your client and seeing or feeling whether or not all of the cords have been severed.

❧ As Michael assists in cutting the cords you will also be cutting them with the ancient healing crystal. Connect in with the deva and wave the crystal across the cords with the intention of severing them. You say:

Send love into the places where the cords have been severed, and spend a few minutes here while your love heals. Now that you are completely free from any old energies and contracts, take a moment to send this person love from deep within your heart. As they send love back into your heart, open and receive. Feel this bond of unconditional love between you.

❧ Hold space while your client receives this unconditional healing love. You say:

> *Visualise* [the name of the person] *dissolving into this golden sphere of light.*

❊ Thank all the beings of light that assisted in this clearing and healing and bring your client back to the present time.

CHAPTER 31

HEALING ANCESTRAL WOUNDS

Healing has several aspects to it, and through life we are offered an opportunity to heal past-life and current-life lessons as well as the lessons and challenges that are handed down the family line. We hold the wounds, suffering, pain and wisdom of those that came before us seven generations forward and back.

Family karma can be described as the emotional pain, trauma, physical diseases, old belief systems and dysfunctional patterning you inherited from your ancestors, your parents, their parents and so on, which continues down the family line for generation after generation until someone awakens to the patterns and heals the pain and suffering that created them and thus gaining strength and wisdom and ending the cycle of the ancestral patterning.

THE MEDICINE OF HEALING ANCESTRAL WOUNDS

We are a product of our environment and we often take on the old beliefs, values and perceptions of our parents. You may hear people expressing things such as 'You have your father's temper' or 'You are so much like your mother', and there is the old saying about the apple not falling far from the tree. These things all highlight this point perfectly. We inherit traits from our parents that can come in the form of physical, emotional, mental or spiritual imbalances or illness and dis-ease. The good news is that you not only hold your family's negative karma but you also hold and have access to the wisdom that has been learned from these lessons and challenges. It is held in your blood and in your bones and is accessible at any time.

As you clear the karmic line and heal and bring awareness to your family karma you receive the gifts of these lessons, challenges and sometimes wounds. The wisdom awakens what has been stored and is dormant within you, and you receive the power and love that comes with this deep healing and understanding. Family or ancestral karma can be healed and released through a range of different processes and techniques. The most powerful way to clear and release yourself from this patterning is via self-awareness: once you see the truth in the old beliefs and patterns that have been handed down you then have the power to heal them.

You can gain deeper awareness by meditating, receiving healing from people who work with family karma or by working with the lords of karma, a group of enlightened beings who assist with releasing karma. It's also encouraged that you work directly with your ancestors in the spirit world, as they are ready and waiting on the other side to assist in your healing. You can create a special altar with photos of your kin and light a candle to honour them and ask for healing.

The shamans and medicine people of the world deeply understood the bond and connection with their ancestors. They focused on strengthening those bonds and healing wounds, facilitating many ceremonies in honour of the ones who walked the land before them and thanking them for their counsel and wisdom. They prayed to and honoured their ancestors seven generations forward and seven generations back, understanding that

their actions would karmically affect their bloodline so they did all they could to keep their bloodline healthy and sacred. They believed that even when their ancestors passed from the earthly plane they still guided and supported them from the spirit world.

MY PERSONAL EXPERIENCE

I came to understand family karma when I went to see an amazing spiritual chiropractor about the slump in the top of my spine. He was very holistic in his approach to healing and offered me a kinesiology session to see why my body was holding in this place. He took me on a journey down through my mother's family tree, guiding me to connect with my grandmother seven generations back and asking me to tune in to what she was doing in her life at that time.

I had to really trust the process. I saw my great-grandmother working the land: she was very stressed and had the weight of the world on her shoulders. My chiropractor told me to see that stress in her daughter and in her daughter's daughter and so on down the family line. He told me to see it in my grandmother in the present time and also in my mother. I saw that my mother also had a slump in her spine and had the huge realisation that the condition was hereditary and that it had come from my ancestors all those many years ago. It was the first time I really understood that energy and karma can continue through a family line.

CRYSTAL ALLIES

AMBER AND
PETRIFIED WOOD

Amber and petrified wood will help you to understand and dissolve the patterns handed down from your family, allowing you to receive love and wisdom from this experience and create a new way of being for yourself and your future ancestors, thus completing the cycle. These two crystals will assist in transforming issues around:

- understanding family karma

- dysfunctional family relationships

- releasing deep-seated family pain and trauma

- healing and transforming old ancestral wounds

- clearing the family line of any further dysfunction.

These two crystals will assist in creating:

- healthy family connections

- an opportunity to honour your ancestors and receive ancestral wisdom and healing

- freedom from your parents' and grandparents' restraints and expectations

- deep mother and father healing.

Amber and petrified wood will support all levels and aspects of healing and the transformation of old ancestral wounds and create a safe loving space.

Amber: creates a deeper connection with nature and tree spirits; draws disease from your body; assists in dissolving old patterns from the past that have been handed down through the family's DNA; and helps to create a deep connection with your ancestors so you can receive their deep wisdom.

Petrified wood: assists in connecting you with tree spirits so you can receive deep wisdom and healing from your ancestors: awakens the deep knowledge that lies within the blood and bones of your ancestry; and helps you to recognise and understand any old ancestral karma brought down through your bloodline.

PRACTITIONER HEALING

Connecting with and healing your ancestors' karma is a truly important part of the healing journey. Due to my own personal life experiences and deep interest in this subject, my understanding is that we receive most of the wounds we bring into adulthood from our childhood directly from our mother and father.

The following healing works deeply and specifically with your parents to help heal these raw and painful wounds and allow for an expanded awareness around your family wounding. It offers an abundance of wisdom, emotional freedom and personal healing to occur.

The first time I was introduced to this type of healing was at a Hay House event facilitated by Denise Linn. I had a profound healing experience around my father and over the years have worked with the essence of this healing, introducing crystals to it and creating my own version of it that I have shared with thousands of people. It is the one I offer here, and I would like to honour Denise Linn for introducing me to this concept. I feel blessed to have been able to share it with so many people.

In this healing you guide your client back in time to before they were born and up into the universe to a sacred place. You invite them to see their mum and dad joining them here. They will work with one parent

at a time to make sure the process is clear and direct. Your client's parents enter into the sacred space at the age of two. There are so many powerful aspects of this healing; however, this part is the most potent.

When your client sees their parents in this young, vulnerable and innocent light there will be a sense of empathy. Your client is given an opportunity to let go of expectations and judgements and realise that at one stage their parents were young and innocent, and they did the best they could with what they knew. Along with the empathy your client will feel unconditional love, which can open them up to start to heal the wounds. They step out of being the wounded child for a moment and see their parents in a different light, which can spark them wanting to comfort and love their parents, not judge them and hold resentment.

The first time I received this healing the experience of meeting my father at such a young age was profound. I saw him as a little boy who just wanted to be loved, and in those moments in the healing I was able to love him unconditionally and let go of all the expectations about what I needed him to be for me. This allowed me to release so much pain I had been holding over the years, as the unconditional love took over my being and created a deep healing. This is why I have chosen to teach and share this healing to this day.

This healing process can be challenging if your client has trauma or conflict around their parents, so it's important to be very gentle in the healing and allow them to go as far as they feel comfortable going. The main energy in this healing is love, so when you guide your client through the process encourage them to send love and intention into their ancestral wounds.

I strongly encourage you to do this healing on yourself first so you are familiar with it and with the energy of the crystals. When you do this healing for yourself, make sure you set up a sacred space and work deeply with the devas of the amber and petrified wood.

- Prepare the healing space by cleansing it.
- Prepare and centre yourself.
- Attune yourself with your client by filling in the client record form (see Chapter 27).
- Make sure you and your client are well hydrated.

⋘ Ask your client to choose 10 crystals to help with the healing, including amber and petrified wood, which you will lay on their chakra points and any other parts of their body you are intuitively guided to. Also choose a few element crystals to assist in bringing balance to the elements within your client's body.

⋘ Set and state out loud your client's intention and add that this healing is for the highest good of all and from the highest place of love possible.

⋘ Invoke guidance from the angels, guides, crystal devas, animal guides and any other beings that you would like to assist in the healing by saying this invocation out loud:

I invoke the love of the divine universe within my heart.
I am a clear and pure channel.
Love is my guide.
I invoke the love of the divine universe within my heart.
I am a clear and pure channel.
Love is my guide.
I invoke the love of the divine universe within my heart
I am a clear and pure channel
Love is my guide.
And I follow that love.

⋘ Bring yourself into your heart centre by connecting with universal love and Mother Earth. Visualise this energy moving through your crown chakra to your heart and down your arms and into your hands. Allow yourself to be a channel of divine love and healing.

⋘ Light sage and guide smoke over your client with a feather. You say:

I ask that the sacred smoke from this sage sends all our prayers and intentions for this healing to our divine creator. I offer you this sacred sage as an honouring of your mind, body and spirit for every breath you have ever taken and for every step you have walked upon this earth. You are blessed.

- Work with the medicine of your drum. Spend five minutes drumming around and over your client, sending love and healing energy. Do this without speaking.

- Work with a feather and set the intention of clearing old energy from the aura as you wave the feather over your client's body to remove and dissolve old energy.

- Place your hands on your client's feet for a few minutes, then their knees, abdomen, heart, the sides of their face and the top of their head. This will allow your client to relax and drop deep into a sacred space of receiving. Do this in silence for five to 10 minutes. Make sure to channel the healing energy of the universe as you open to be a pure channel.

- Guide your client to connect deeply with the universe, earth and crystals. You say:

Visualise a beautiful golden light streaming down from the heavens and into the top of your head. Feel this healing light move into your heart and allow your heart to pulsate this light through your whole body and into every single cell of your being.

- Guide your client using your own words to connect deeply with the golden healing light of the universe and send it through their body and into every cell of their being.

- Guide your client to connect with Mother Earth. You say:

Visualise a root extending down from the bottom of your spine. Send this root deep into the earth, down, down, deep down into the centre of the earth. Anchor your roots into the heart of Mother Gaia. She becomes aware of your presence, and she sends you her loving, nurturing, nourishing, healing energy. Breathe this up into your spine and into your heart. Allow your heart to send this healing energy into the rest of your body.

* Guide your client using your own words to receive the love and blessings of the earth.
* Guide your client to connect deeply with the crystals by encouraging them to take very long, deep breaths for five minutes. As they breathe and connect, play a crystal bowl to amplify energy and say the following:

Bring your awareness to your heart. On your in breath, breathe the energy of the universe and the earth into your heart. On your out breath, send this energy out to the crystals. On your next in breath, breathe the energy of the crystals into your heart. On your next out breath, send this crystal healing energy into every cell of your being.

Use your own words and listen to your intuition to facilitate your client's deep connection with the crystals and sending this energy into their body. Make sure you encourage them to take long, deep breaths to amplify the healing energy.

You will now guide your client to undertake a healing journey. You say:

Journey back to a recent memory of your life from earlier today, and allow yourself to feel the memory as if it is happening now. Immerse yourself in it, then let it go.

Journey to a memory from last week, and feel it as though it is happening now. Let it go.

Travel back in time slowly and gently to when you were eighteen, seventeen, sixteen, fifteen, fourteen, thirteen, twelve, eleven, ten, nine, eight, seven, six, five, four, three, two, one, six months old, three months, one month old: all the way back in time, travelling back, back into the womb, travelling back beyond, back, back into the universe.

Take your spirit to a beautiful garden; take a moment to arrive here in this sacred space. As you look around you see an abundance of prettily coloured flowers and hundreds of butterflies dancing around. You then see in the distance a small bench, and you are invited to sit down there and take a moment to drink in the bliss of this peaceful place.

You now see in the distance a small child running towards you, and realise this is your mother at a young age. She is running towards you with her arms open, calling for you.

Gently embrace your mother and put her on your lap. Comfort her and nurture her as you would a child in need. Let her know she is loved and cared for. Take a few moments to be together.

Understand that your mother was once a little girl who felt scared and lost at times and required love, and see her innocence and vulnerability.

We now call in the devas of petrified wood and amber, and I invite you to breathe in the healing energy of these crystals into your heart.

Imagine the light of the universe and this powerful crystal energy surrounding you both, a light of love and wisdom, and feel and see the light weave all the way through your mother's life. See the

light supporting your mum through her life, always protected and loved.

See the light making its way into your mother's womb, joining you as a little baby before you were born. As you enter into this world, see this light of love surround you. See it travel with you, guiding you throughout your life and all the way up to the present time as you feel completely supported and loved. Feel this healing light of the universe and the crystals permeate every cell of your being. Feel it healing any old wounds as you invite this light of love into the present moment and into your consciousness right here and now. Stay here for a while as you deeply receive this energy.

It is now time to tune in to any old beliefs, patterns, illness or family karma that you may be holding that has been handed down through your family's DNA. Take a few moments as you gather this energy into a ball from your mind, body and spirit. You don't have to know exactly what the karma is; just setting the intention is strong enough.

It is now time to hand this karmic energy back down the family line to where it first started. We call upon your ancestors in the spirit world to be present and to receive these old patterns. We ask that as this energy returns to you, you transmute it to love and wisdom.

Start to hand the energy back with love to your mother. See your mother receive this energy and then hand it back to where it came from, all the way down the family line.

Your ancestors receive this energy and transform it into love and wisdom. They now send this love and wisdom back down the family line and your mum offers it to you. Open and receive the love and wisdom from your ancestors. Stay here for a few minutes and open to this energy fully.

Once you have integrated this energy see yourself handing this wisdom, light and healing down to your children and to your children's children. Send it seven generations forward.

Take a moment to thank your ancestors for sharing in your healing today.

Take yourself back to the sacred healing garden where you first started and see your mother sitting on your lap once more. This time she feels content and happy and she runs off into the distance with joy and love in her heart and you see her dissolve in a beautiful golden light.

Repeat the process with your client's father, starting at the sacred garden, although this time your client's father runs towards you as you sit on the bench. You say:

You now see in the distance a small child running towards you and realise this is your father at a young age. He is running towards you with his arms open, calling for you.

Gently embrace your father and put him on your lap. Comfort him and nurture him as you would a child in need. Let him know he is loved and cared for. Take a few moments to be together.

Understand that your father was once a little boy who felt scared and lost at times and required love. See his innocence and vulnerability.

We now call in the devas of petrified wood and amber, and I invite you to breathe the healing energy of these crystals into your heart.

Imagine the light of the universe and the crystal energy surrounding you both, a light of love and wisdom, and feel and see the light weave all the way through your father's life. See the light supporting him through his life, always protected and loved. Your father meets

your mum, and then after some time you are born. As you enter into this world, see this light of love surround you. See it travel with you, guiding you throughout your life all the way up to the present time as you feel completely supported and loved. Feel this healing light of the universe and the crystals permeate every cell of your being. Feel it healing any old wounds as you invite this light of love into the present moment and into your consciousness, right here and now. Stay here for a while as you receive this energy deeply.

It is now time to tune in to any old beliefs, patterns, illness or family karma you may be holding that has been handed down through your family DNA. Take a few moments as you gather this energy into a ball from your mind, body and spirit. You don't have to know exactly what the karma is; just setting the intention is strong enough.

It is now time to hand this karmic energy back down the family line to where it first started. We call upon your ancestors in the spirit world to be present and receive these old patterns. We ask that as this energy returns to you, you transmute it to love and wisdom.

Start to hand the energy back with love to your father. See him receive this energy as he hands it back to where it came from, all the way down the family line. Your ancestors receive this energy and transform it into love and wisdom. They send this love and wisdom back down the family line and now your father offers it to you. Open and receive the love and wisdom from your ancestors. Stay here for a few minutes and open to this energy fully.

Once you have integrated this energy, see yourself handing this wisdom, light and healing down to your children and to your children's children. Send it seven generations forward.

Take a moment to thank your ancestors for sharing in your healing today.

Take yourself back to the sacred healing garden where you first started and see your father sitting on your lap once more. This time he feels content and happy and runs off into the distance with joy and love in his heart. Now see him dissolve in a beautiful golden light.

Once you have facilitated the healing for your client's mother and father:

* You say:

It is time to return to the present. Allow the memories to fade away and feel strong and empowered as you return.

This journey has allowed deep healing with your ancestors and has enriched the lives of you all.

* Finish the healing by placing your hands on your client's head and sending love into their being. Next, place your hands on your client's feet and set the intention to bring your client back into their body and into the now.

* Use a drum or bells to close the healing as you direct this sound over your client's body.

* Gently bring your client back into the room and fully back into their body. Bring their conscious awareness to the present moment: right here, right now.

* Ask your client to thank their ancestors, guides, angels, crystal devas, animal spirits and any other being that assisted in the healing.

❧ Suggest to your client they create a sacred alter for their ancestors as an offering and honouring of the healing. Invite them to find a photo of their ancestors and place it somewhere special in their home and light a candle for them for the next three days.

❧ Fill in the client record form (see Chapter 27).

❧ Cleanse your crystals and separate yourself from the healing.

PART VII

SELF-CARE
AND
NURTURING

CHAPTER 32

CREATING A PERSONALISED SELF-CARE SCHEDULE

As you embark upon a healing journey for yourself and others it is super important to look after yourself on all levels. Self-care is essential. Healers love to nurture and care for others and have truly mastered the art of giving. Being of service sparks a passion inside and a sense of fulfilling their purpose.

Unfortunately, though, many healers forget to give back to themselves and can find it challenging to receive. It is extremely important as you walk the path of a medicine person to practise giving unconditional love to yourself. It might not come as easily as giving to others, but it's a critical part of self-care and should become a part of your day-to-day schedule to prevent burn out and exhaustion.

There are many things you can do to care and nurture yourself, and a great way to start is by making a list. To get balance and more of a holistic outcome it's a good idea to list your actions in four categories: mental, physical, emotional and spiritual. Under each category, write a list of the things you love doing that nurture your soul and make you feel good; here are some examples to get you started.

Physical:

- walking dogs on the beach
- dancing
- yoga
- swimming
- receiving a massage
- eating healthily
- going to the gym
- gardening
- walking in nature.

Mental:

- conscious breathing
- drawing
- reading
- journaling
- crossword puzzles
- meditating.

Emotional:

- playing with your crystals
- talking to a friend
- breath work
- keeping a gratitude diary
- playing with your children or animals
- receiving a healing.

Spiritual:

- self-healing
- prayer
- meditation
- undertaking ceremonies
- trance drumming.

Create a personalised self-care list.

PHYSICAL: _____

_____

MENTAL: _____

_____

EMOTIONAL: _____

_____

SPIRITUAL: _____

_____

Now that you have a self-care list you need to allocate time for your planned activities in your daily schedule. A good start is to allocate at least five minutes per day to each category, as it's best to begin with short amounts of time that are achievable and slowly add on extra time once you feel committed. It won't take long to feel the results from this self-love, which will inspire you to spend more time doing those things you love.

Fill in the weekly schedule below with one thing from each category on your list for each day. Keep the same schedule for a month to make it easy for you and to help create some momentum and stability with it. Once you're able to stay committed and get on a roll you can mix up your plan and add in more from your list or swap them out for other things you love doing. The most important thing is that you enjoy what you're doing and make it fun. Print out the schedule and place it on the fridge or in a spot where you're going to see it each day to remind you to constantly offer these goodies to yourself.

MONDAY: _____

_____

TUESDAY: _____

_____

WEDNESDAY: _____

_____

THURSDAY: _____

_____

FRIDAY: _____

_____

SATURDAY: _____

_____

SUNDAY: _____

A FEW FINAL WORDS

Thank you for taking this sacred journey with me as you awaken the shaman within. Hopefully my stories invoked your own powerful memories and deep connection with yourself and your own unique, sacred, personal medicine, and the healings, ceremonies and wisdom have sparked a deep healing and awakening of your soul. You are a part of the rainbow bridges, and I invite you to join me as we come together as one people, one voice, one heart, one love for the greater good of humanity. We have ventured so far away from ourselves, from each other, all living beings and this sacred land, and it is time to take the journey back home to this deep connection once again.

My prayer is that you have gained an abundance of wisdom, healing, connection and confidence so you can continue to work with and offer your gifts to yourself, others and the world, that you have experienced a deep remembering of who you are and your mission here on earth. May you continue to walk gently on this precious land, be kind, compassionate and understanding to yourself and others, and may you continue to connect

with earth medicine and your spirit team and offer this love and healing to the world for the greater good of all humanity.

I would like to thank all of your guides, members of your spirit team and your ancestors for holding space while you took the sacred journey within. I also offer a huge acknowledgement and heartfelt thank you to you – yes, you – for doing the sometimes challenging but definitely worth it personal healing work and for choosing the path of love as you shine your light to make this world a better place. May you journey safe and enjoy this global awakening back to your heart, your truth, to the oneness of all that is and the sacred divine Mother Earth. I hope one day our paths cross in the physical, but until then be kind and well and thank you once again for sharing this sacred journey with me. May you forever walk with peace in your heart and soul.

Love and blessings

Rachelle

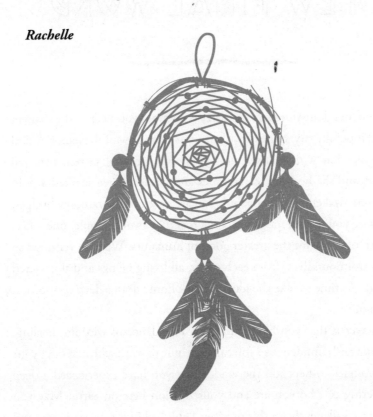

ACKNOWLEDGEMENTS

I am truly blessed to have had such a powerful awakening into my shamanic wisdom and hold all the earthly medicines and their guardians deeply in my heart. I would like to express my gratitude to everyone who has come into my life and shared so freely their love, wisdom and support, which has held and guided me on my path to help others.

A special thank you to my fiancé for always being by my side, for loving me for who I am and for helping me write this book. You are the grounding presence in my life. I'd also like to thank my spirit team, especially my old wise owl woman, whom I believe to be a higher aspect of my soul and the keeper of wisdom for this book and who guides me on all my shamanic journeys. I am forever grateful for you all.

ABOUT THE AUTHOR

Rachelle Charman's medicine and teachings flow naturally from the heart, driven by her love of humanity and passion for assisting people to awaken to their soul's calling. She is recognised globally for her depth and authenticity, and is a dynamic, passionate teacher and healer who travels the world with her teachings, paving the way for others to connect with their own innate healing wisdom.

Rachelle's soul awakening happened in 2000, when she had a profound healing experience with a crystal that set her on the path of health and healing. Her biggest teacher is life itself, along with the potent medicine of the earth, spirit, universal consciousness and love. Throughout her journey she has spent time with Peruvian shamans and native healers in the Amazon, where she witnessed and experienced profound healings and gained much insight into the healing ways of the native tribes. This ignited her memories and inner knowledge of shamanic and crystal healing.

Rachelle lives in Byron Bay, Australia with her fiancé and two beautiful labradors. She continues to travel the world as a master healer and inspirational speaker, sharing stories from her life to help others on their path of self-love and self-mastery.

RACHELLECHARMAN.COM

CRYSTAL
SHAMANISM